メガトー
megatokyo

5

Fred Gallagher & Larry Berry – Design
Jim Chadwick – Editor

ISBN:1-4012-1127-5
ISBN-13: 978-1-4012-1127-1

メガトーキョー
megatokyo

5

by
FRED GALLAGHER

"leave it to seraphim" comics written by
SARAH GALLAGHER

"shirt guy dom" comics by
DOMINIC NGUYEN

www.megatokyo.com

CMX

cmxmanga.com

A special thanks to:

Mohammad F. Haque (Hawk) who colored the cover image
and helped me process much of the material in this book.

Ray Kremer and Warren Bailey for their help with typo
checking and gathering material for the Readers' Guide.

Dom for going yet another year without capping me.

And Sarah, without whom I wouldn't be able to do any of this.

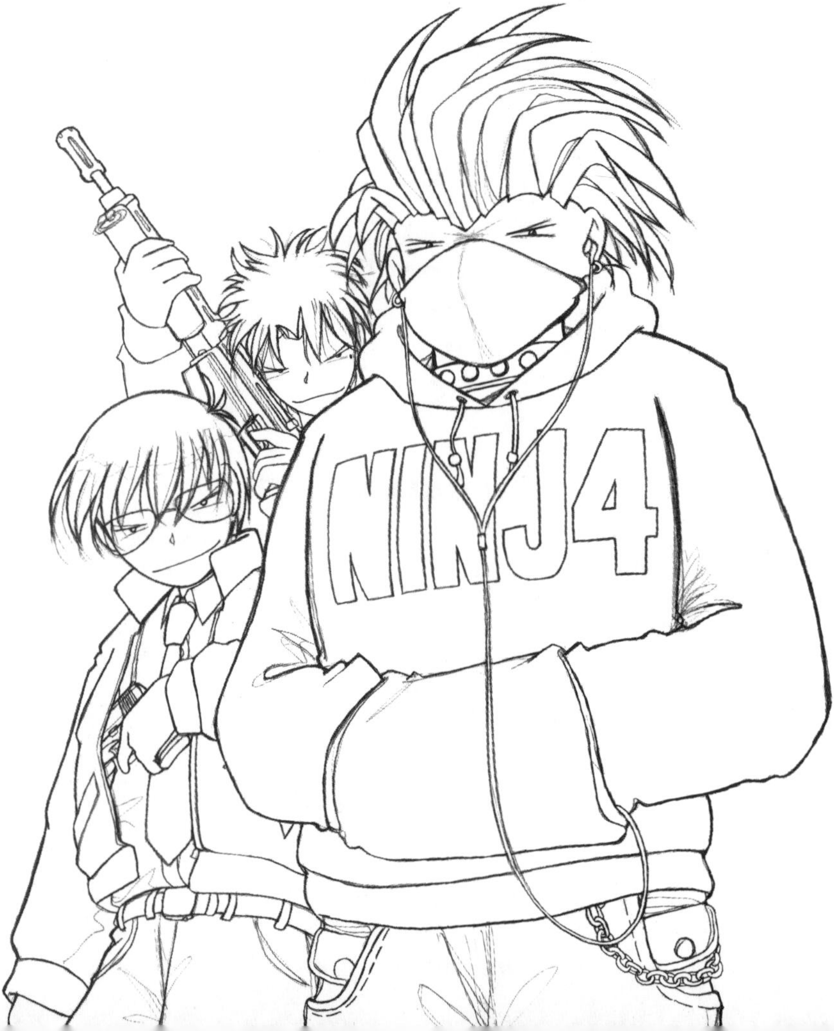

CONTENTS

MT_vol_5_fr33talk.txt

Hi and welcome to *Megatokyo* volume 5.

If you've been a regular online reader of *Megatokyo* for the past few years, you are probably aware of how much time it takes for me to pull one of these books together. Most of you are supportive (or simply resigned) to the fact that when I am working on a *Megatokyo* collection, there will be weeks of missed comics and a general lack of content for the website. Even though you folks are patient, I always feel pressured to finish things as quick as possible so I can get back to making comics.

Book processing can be a miserable pressure cooker. It's like digging into the past and having to reconcile all of your sins of assembly and do penance for a quirky creative workflow. In recent years I've been doing a better job of assembling comics in ways that make it easier to process them for print, but it still takes time. No matter how much you do up front, 240 pages is a lot of material deal with.

I try not to whine or gripe too much, but after several weeks of working on nothing but the book, I find myself frustrated, irritated and *so* ready to be done. I've felt like this all week. Hopefully, when I start the next chapter, some of the changes I'm making to my workflow will make things easier when I pull together my next book...

My "next" book?

There are four *Megatokyo* books sitting on my desk. I'm griping about finishing up my fifth book, which goes to press in a few weeks.

Five published books.

Huh.

tak
tak
tak
tak
tak
tak

MT_vol_5_fr33talk.txt

Have you ever played one of those crazy motocross or driving arcade games where you zip along on these dizzying, insane, physically impossible courses? All of your attention is focused on looking ahead and trying not to crash. The last thing on your mind is looking at the path you just traversed. *Megatokyo* feels like that sometimes. I'm so busy trying to keep up with the next crazy jump or steep descent that that I never feel like I have the luxury to review where I've been.

I have to admit, it was kinda weird when it dawned on me that I haven't just done one or two books, but five.

Years and years ago, when I first started to think about creating manga-inspired work, there wasn't much of a market for it here in the States. When Rodney Caston (the co-creator of *Megatokyo* who I worked with until 2002) approached me about doing a webcomic, I agreed to do it partly because I realized that it was one of the best ways to reach potential readers. I was wary of doing monthlies, and books were kind of out of the question. Comic book shops were not the place where people who might be interested in work like mine tended to frequent, and as for bookstores...yeah, right, like Borders would ever carry manga. :P

Amazing how things change, isn't it? The popularity of manga and anime in the States has grown exponentially, providing a market for work like mine that I never thought possible. Seven years, five published books, working full time creating comics for a living, having a successful online store run by Sarah and myself, being picked up by DC Comics and having one of the best-selling English language manga titles in the world... It's kinda mind boggling when I stop to think about it, and there's stuff on the horizon I can't even tell you about yet.

Longtime readers who are used to my rather negative and self-deprecating way of talking about my work are probably wondering, "Who are you, and what have you done with Fred?"

tak
tak
tak
nyow?
tak
tak
tak

MT_vol_5_fr33talk.txt

It takes a lot to make me feel like I've done OK. When I'm mired in little errors and find out that I forgot to toggle off "sharpening" in a Photoshop action ruining a dozen or so processed files, or when I'm stuck on a single line of dialogue and can't get a drawing to work...it's easy to feel like nothing is going right or I have no idea what I'm doing.

Looking at these five books, the plethora of supportive emails, all of the drawings I've done for people at conventions, the sheer volume of people who visit the *Megatokyo* site each and every day and the response I get from readers all over the world...it's hard for me to maintain my excessive negativity. I still insist that my work sucks and is nowhere near up to standards I set for myself, but for some reason, most people seem to be OK with it. They get it, they understand, and they forgive me.

So maybe it's not so bad, even if there is a lot of room for improvement.

At the back of this book you will find a Readers' Guide, which is something that I've needed to put together for a long time. I engaged the help of two friends and long-time MT fans, Ray Kremer and Warren Bailey, to help me pull the material together for this guide. The world of *Megatokyo* is pretty complicated, and even I have trouble getting my head around it sometimes. I suppose it's only fair to try to give new readers a fighting chance of understanding what is going on.

Thanks for reading, and I hope you enjoy this book.

piro

tak
tak
tak
tak
tak
tak
claw
claw

メガトーキョー
megatokyo
chapter 7:
"known bugs and security flaws"
デニーズ
Denny's
MISSED YOU AT BREAKFAST YESTERDAY.
YOU TAKE A SICK DAY?
YEAH. I HAD TO SPEND A LITTLE MORE TIME THAN USUAL IN THE GROWTH TANK.
SOMETHING TO DO WITH BEING REDUCED TO TRACE AMOUNTS OF DUST ON TWO COTTON SWABS.
GAPU.
FEH. I'M SURE YOUR LAB PEOPLE TOOK THEIR TIME JUST TO ANNOY YOU.
KINDA LOOKS LIKE THEY GAVE YOU A WHOLE NEW HEAD.
MUCH BETTER. MY URGE TO SHOOT YOU IN THE FACE ISN'T QUITE SO STRONG NOW.
IT'S A HEAD. IT WORKS.
AS LONG AS IT CAN EXPRESS HOW MUCH I ENJOY KILLING PEOPLE, IT'S ALL GOOD.
AND TO THINK ALL I HAVE IS AN OPTICAL PLAN.
I THINK MY EGGS ARE TICKING.
HOW DOES MY "I REALLY LOVE TO BLOW STUFF UP" EXPRESSION LOOK?

WHOOM!
<THANK YOU! PLEASE COME AGAIN!>
AHH... SUCH A NICE DAY.
HAVOC IS ALWAYS BEST STARTED ON NICE DAYS.
HOW'S THE TAKEDOWN OF THAT E.D.S. PROTOTYPE GOING?
I'VE HAD A FEW SETBACKS. NOTHING SERIOUS. I'LL FINISH IT TODAY.
WHY DIDN'T YOU SNAG IT WHILE I WAS OUT? SCARED OF A LITTLE PLASTIC GIRLIE?
NOT INTERESTED. SEGA GOT OUT OF THE CONSOLE BIZ, WE'RE INTO CREATING CONTENT NOW, REMEMBER?
OH YEAH, YOU'RE AFTER THAT LEVEL 9 EX-IDOL.
SHE'S TAGGED WITH AT LEAST THIRTY HAZARD MARKERS.
CORPORATE WON'T LET ME GO NEAR HER.
BUT THAT'S WHAT MAKES IT CHALLENGING.
AH... THE CONSOLE BIZ.
BACK WHEN SEGA WAS STILL IN THE GAME, REMEMBER HOW MUCH FUN WE HAD?
THE BATTLES? THE CARNAGE? THE FUN?
YEAH.
NINTENDO STILL CAN'T FIND ANYONE TO REPLACE THAT GUY WE CHUNKED WHEN I WAS "PROMOTING" THE DREAMCAST. SEEMS NO ONE WANTS HIS JOB.
WUSSES.

WELL, IT'S BOOTING UP...
AND IT HASN'T BURST INTO FLAMES YET.
THAT'S PROMISING.
HNNNNNNNNNNNNNNNNNNNNNNNNNNN
AND...
IT WORKS. AMA-ZING.
IT IS THE BEST I CAN DO WITH THE PARTS I COULD SALVAGE.
HEY, THANKS, DUDE. I'VE MISSED HAVING A COMPUTER OF MY OWN.
SO, I GUESS THE NEXT THING WE NEED TO DO IS TEST MY "CEREAL BOX SPECIAL" AGAINST YOUR MOSTLY BURNED OUT--
IT CAN WAIT.
I AM IN NEED OF AIR.
tsubasa: PIRO-SAN!
piro: hey! tsubasa!! you're alive! where are you?
tsubasa: I am in Iowa.
piro: IOWA?
tsubasa: Yes, are you home now?
piro: no, we're still in Tokyo.
tsubasa: you are?
piro: yeah, it's a long story.
tsubasa: how is largo-san?
piro: well, he just built me a pc out of a cereal box and spare parts, but he did it without taking off any of his clothes and when he was done he said he needed some air and went outside.
tsubasa: ...
tsubasa: have you called for ambulance?
piro: no, no, i think he's just got a bit of a... hangover.
tsubasa: i call ambulance for you!

<EXCUSE ME, HAYASAKA-SAN?>
<CAN I HAVE YOUR AUTO-GRAPH?>
GAMERS
<OH, UM... SURE.>

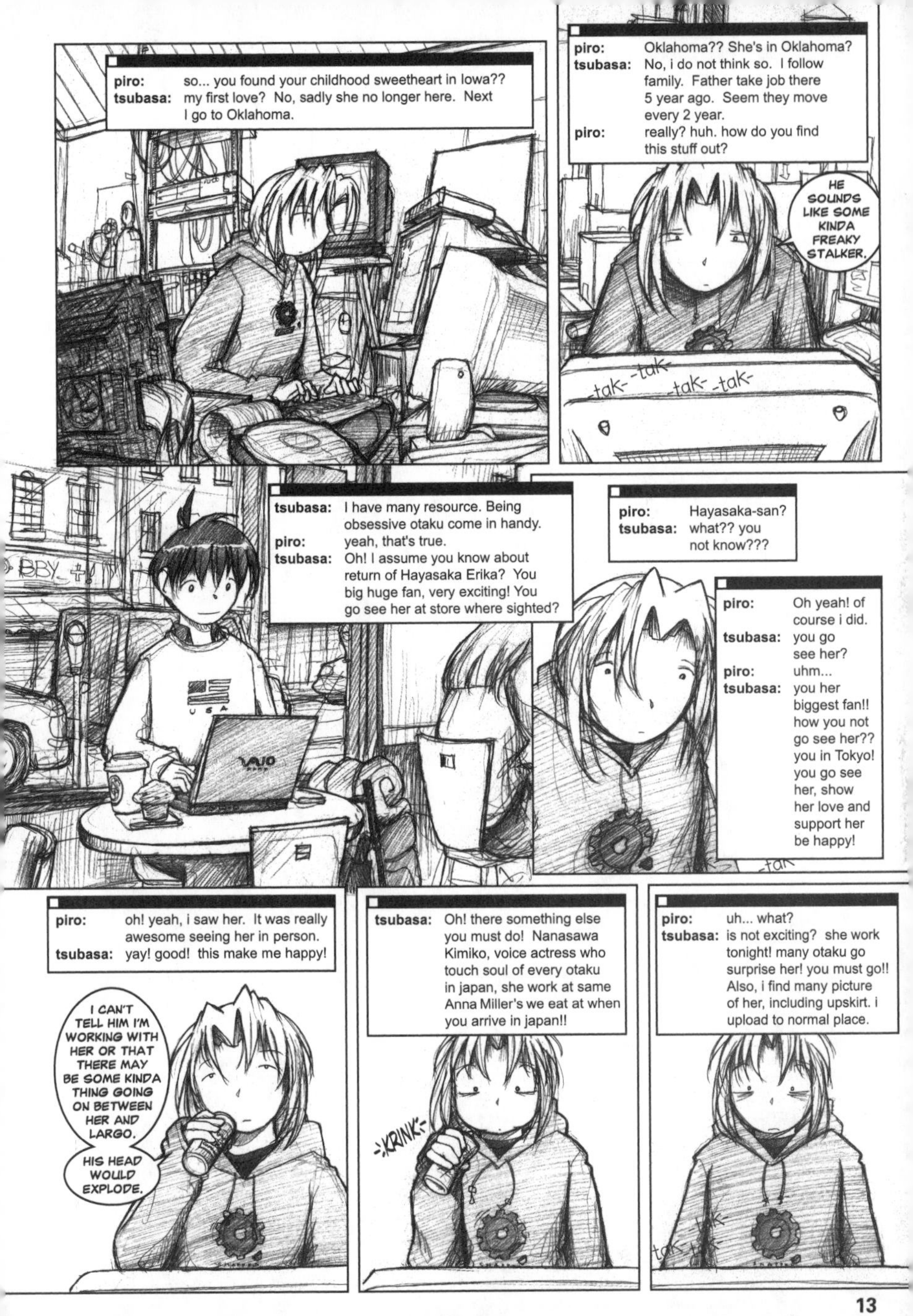

piro: so... you found your childhood sweetheart in Iowa??
tsubasa: my first love? No, sadly she no longer here. Next I go to Oklahoma.
piro: Oklahoma?? She's in Oklahoma?
tsubasa: No, i do not think so. I follow family. Father take job there 5 year ago. Seem they move every 2 year.
piro: really? huh. how do you find this stuff out?
HE SOUNDS LIKE SOME KINDA FREAKY STALKER.
-tak- -tak- -tak- -tak-
tsubasa: I have many resource. Being obsessive otaku come in handy.
piro: yeah, that's true.
tsubasa: Oh! I assume you know about return of Hayasaka Erika? You big huge fan, very exciting! You go see her at store where sighted?
piro: Hayasaka-san?
tsubasa: what?? you not know???
piro: Oh yeah! of course i did.
tsubasa: you go see her?
piro: uhm...
tsubasa: you her biggest fan!! how you not go see her?? you in Tokyo! you go see her, show her love and support her be happy!
-tak
piro: oh! yeah, i saw her. It was really awesome seeing her in person.
tsubasa: yay! good! this make me happy!
I CAN'T TELL HIM I'M WORKING WITH HER OR THAT THERE MAY BE SOME KINDA THING GOING ON BETWEEN HER AND LARGO.
HIS HEAD WOULD EXPLODE.
tsubasa: Oh! there something else you must do! Nanasawa Kimiko, voice actress who touch soul of every otaku in japan, she work at same Anna Miller's we eat at when you arrive in japan!!
KRINK
piro: uh... what?
tsubasa: is not exciting? she work tonight! many otaku go surprise her! you must go!! Also, i find many picture of her, including upskirt. i upload to normal place.

piro: Nanasawa? Nanasawa Kimiko??
tsubasa: Yes! Voice actress for Kotone in "Sight." She say wonderful things on Mumu-chan's Voice Voice Paradise, touch everyone's hearts. did you not listen last night??
piro: uh, no... What did she say?
tsubasa wah! I upload mp3 of show and transcript! You listen!!!
-tak-
-tak-
-tak-
-tak-
tsubasa: after listen, come to channel, we all talk about her!
piro: uh, what channel?
tsubasa: any channel!! Be sure you look at pictures. she *very* cute, make heart stop. she type girl *you* like very much!! small breast but shapely leg
piro: GTG!
[piro has disconnected]
-tak-
-tak-
-tak-
OK, THAT WAS... WEIRD.
TSUBASA'S RIGHT. EVERYONE IS TALKING ABOUT KIMIKO-SAN. WHAT THE HELL DID SHE SAY ON THAT RADIO SHOW??
LET'S SEE IF HE FINISHED UPLOADING THE--
WAH? TSUBASA REALLY DID FIND AN UPSKIRT PIC?
NO WAY...
WELL, YOU GONNA ADMIRE THE FILENAME OR ARE YOU GONNA CLICK ON IT SO WE CAN CHECK OUT THE GOODS?

WHAT?? NO!! I HAVE NO INTENTION OF LOOKING AT THAT PICTURE!!
WHAT KIND OF PERSON DO YOU THINK I AM??
NO!!
A SLIGHTLY LESS THAN HEALTHY YOUNG MAN.
NOW GET WITH THE CLICKIN'.
HEY, DON'T TELL ME YOU DON'T WANNA GET UP THIS CHICK'S SKIRT. WHAT'S WRONG WITH TAKIN' A PEEK LIKE EVERYONE ELSE?
THERE'S PLENTY WRONG WITH IT!!
WHAT'S WITH THE HUFFY "OH, I'D **NEVER** DO THAT!" SCHTICK? YOU DON'T HAVE TO ACT INNOCENT AROUND ME.
WE BOTH KNOW YOU'RE GONNA LOOK.
NO, I AM NOT.
WOW, YOU **SO** NEED A GIRLFRIEND.
WHAT? HOW THE HELL DO YOU KNOW I DON'T HAVE ONE??
IT'S KINDA OBVIOUS. IT ALWAYS IS.
WHAT'S WRONG, PIRO?
IT'S JUST... KIMIKO-SAN. ALL THIS TALK ABOUT HER, FINDING OUT WHERE SHE WORKS, SOMEONE SNEAKING AN UPSKIRT PICTURE OF HER.
THAT'S... REALLY BAD.
DOES SHE KNOW ABOUT ALL OF THIS?
SHOULD I TELL HER?
AND YOU'RE AFRAID THAT IF YOU TELL HER, ESPECIALLY ABOUT THE PICTURE, SHE'LL WONDER WHAT YOU WERE DOING TO COME ACROSS THEM IN THE FIRST PLACE, RIGHT?
OH. I... HADN'T THOUGHT ABOUT THAT.
SEE HOW INNOCENT HE IS?
FEH. HE CAN AT LEAST LET **ME** LOOK.

★breeebree★
★breeebr-
<THAT'S THE FOURTH TIME HE'S TRIED TO CALL THIS MORNING.>
<REHHH... I'M NOT READY TO TALK TO HIM YET.>
SIGH <LIKE I'LL EVER BE.>
<I GUESS I SHOULD STOP AVOIDING IT...>
<AND CALL HIM.>
<GUTS, KIMIKO! GUTS! MAKE THE CALL!>
-BREEBREE!- -BREEBREE!- -BRE--
<ALL I HAVE TO DO IS SAY HI, THEN-->
<NANASAWA!!! WHERE THE HELL HAVE YOU BEEN?!?>
<WHY HAVEN'T YOU BEEN ANSWERING YOUR PHONE???>
<I, I-->
<ALL HELL IS BREAKING LOOSE BECAUSE OF THAT STUNT YOU PULLED LAST NIGHT!>
<UWAHH!! I'M SORRY! I'M SORRY I'M SORRY!!!>
<MATSUI, STOP, YOU'LL SCARE THE POOR THING.>
<GIVE ME THE PHONE.>
<SO, NANASAWA, HOW DOES IT FEEL TO BE AN OVERNIGHT SENSATION?>
<UWEH? A WHAT?>
<YOU SHOULD PROBABLY COME DOWN HERE BEFORE MATSUI HAS A SEIZURE.>
<OH, I REMEMBER YOUR AGENT SAYING THAT YOU COULD SING.>
<BRING YOUR DEMO TAPES, I'D LIKE TO HEAR THEM.>
<REEHHHHH????>

CRAP! BOSS-SAN WANTED ME TO OPEN UP THIS MORNING BECAUSE HAYASAKA-SAN HAS TODAY OFF. I'M ALREADY TWENTY MINUTES LATE! I HOPE NO ONE IS--
<THANK YOU, THANK YOU, HAYASAKA-SAMA!!>
EEP!
<YOU ARE VERY WELCOME.>
<TAKE CARE.>
<H...HAYASAKA-SAN? I THOUGHT BOSS-SAN SAID-->
<THERE ISN'T ANYONE ELSE IN THE STORE, IS THERE?>
<ER, NO, NOT THAT I COULD SEE.>
<GOOD.>
<I'M TIRED OF SMILING.>
<HAYASAKA-SAN...>
<YOUR PHONE.>
<WHA?>
<YOUR CELL PHONE IS RINGING.>
-brreeeee-
<OH! RIGHT. SORRY...>
<WHA? KIMIKO-SAN?!>
-brreeeee-
-brreeeee-
<WHY IS SHE...>
<CALLING...>
<...?>
-brreeeee-
-brreeeee-
<WELL, YOU COULD ANSWER THE PHONE AND ASK HER.>
-brreeeee-
-brreeeee-

UH...
-brreeeee-
-brreeeee-
<EXCUSE ME, JUST FOR A MOMENT.>
-brreeeee-
-brreeeee-
<WOULD YOU LIKE SOME COFFEE? WE HAVE EXTRA.>
<NO THANK YOU.>
<HELLO? KIMIKO-SAN! HOW ARE-->
<WHAT? WHAT'S WRONG??>
<SO, ARE YOU REALLY INTERESTED IN LEARNING HOW TO DRAW, OR DO YOU JUST HAVE SOME KIND OF PUBESCENT INFATUATION WITH OLDER, BLOND AMERICAN BOYS?>
<I'M IN SO MUCH TROUBLE!!>
<TROUBLE? WHAT HAPPENED? ARE YOU OK?>
<SAYURI-SAN SAYS I MADE A HUGE IMPRESSION ON MUMU-CHAN'S LISTENERS WITH WHAT I SAID ABOUT FANBOYS AND OTAKU. SHE SAYS I'VE TURNED INTO SOME KIND OF INSTANT CELEBRITY!!>
<I KNOW! IT'S ALL OVER THE NET! DOZENS OF FAN PAGES DEVOTED TO YOU, AND EVERYONE IS TALKING ABOUT WHAT YOU SAID ON-->
<H...HOW CAN YOU ASK SOMETHING LIKE THAT SO PLAINLY?!?>
<IT'S A VALID QUESTION. HOW ABOUT A DONUT? THEY'RE FRESH.>
<THEY ARE? ONLINE? ON THE INTERNET?>
<YEAH, AND YOU CAN EVEN DOWNLOAD THE SHOW AND LISTEN-->
<REHHHHHHH?!? YOU HAVEN'T LISTENED TO IT, HAVE YOU? HAVE YOU? PLEASE SAY YOU HAVEN'T LISTENED TO IT!!>
<NANASAWA-SAN, CALM DOWN, CALM DOWN!!>

<WELL?>
<I DOWNLOADED IT, BUT I HAVEN'T LISTENED TO IT!>
<YOU HAVEN'T?>
<NO, AND IF YOU DON'T WANT ME TO, I WON'T.>
<PROMISE?>
<I PROMISE.>
<I... WANT TO LEARN... HOW HE DOES IT.>
<DOES WHAT?>
<HOW HE DRAWS HIS FEELINGS.>
<ALL I'VE DONE IS READ WHAT PEOPLE HAVE BEEN SAYING, THAT'S ALL.>
<WHAT ARE THEY SAYING?>
<IT'S ALL GOOD! THEY ARE SAYING THAT YOU UNDERSTAND THEM AND CARE ABOUT THEIR FEELINGS.>
<ON THE OUTSIDE HE SEEMS SO PLAIN, BORING AND STUPID, BUT SOMETHING ELSE... COMES OUT IN HIS DRAWINGS.>
<I WANT TO BE ABLE TO DO THAT.>
<TO EXPRESS WHAT I FEEL INSIDE. FEELINGS YOU CAN'T DESCRIBE ANY OTHER WAY.>
<WHATEVER YOU SAID, IT MADE A LOT OF PEOPLE REALLY HAPPY. THEY'RE PRACTICALLY WORSHIPING YOU.>
<THEY'RE WORSHIPING ME... BECAUSE I FEEL SORRY FOR THEM?>
<THAT'S... HORRIBLE!>
<I'M NOT SURE I'D WANT TO KNOW HIS INNER FEELINGS IF HE SAW ME IN A SKIRT THAT SHORT.>
<IT'S NOT SHORT!!!>
SKRTSH!
<HORRIBLE? WHY IS IT HORRIBLE? YOU DO CARE, AND I THINK THAT MEANS A LOT TO THEM.>
<BUT... I CAN'T CARE ABOUT THAT MANY PEOPLE, PIRO-SAN! I CAN'T!!>

<BUT KIMIKO-SAN, YOU ALREADY DO!>
<THAT'S WHAT YOU WERE TALKING ABOUT LAST NIGHT, RIGHT?>
<UHNN... WELL...>
BEEP! BEEP!
FLUMP
<WAH? MATSUI-SAN? AGAIN??>
<PIRO-SAN? I HAVE TO GO! MATSUI-SAN IS CALLING ME!>
<I... I'LL CALL YOU BACK?>
<SURE! I'LL BE HERE! GOOD LUCK!!>
<SORRY ABOUT THAT! HEH.>
<TALKING TO YOUR GIRL-FRIEND?>
<EH? MY, MY-->
<IF YOU'RE STILL LOOKING TO AVOID GIVING HER DRAWING LESSONS, NOW WOULD BE THE TIME TO RUN.>
<WHAT? NO! I'M SO SORRY I KEEP MISSING ALL OF YOUR LESSONS, SUN... SAN... SOU...>
<SONODA!! SONODA YUKI!!!>
<IT'S NOT A HARD NAME TO REMEMBER!!>
<WAH!! I'M SO SORRY SONODA-SAN!! I'M TERRIBLE WITH NAMES!>
<SONODA YUKI??>
<GOT A PROBLEM WITH MY NAME?>

WHUP WHUP WHUP
KAA!
RAWR!!
<LIGHT BLUE-GREEN RANGER, FLYING MONKEY POSITION!!>
<PINK WITH SPARKLES RANGER, FIST OF DEFIANCE POSITION!!>
<MAUVE RANGER, FETAL POSITION!!>
<FEED ON THIS, VILE BEAST!!>
<LOOK OUT!>
hiissssss!!!
KLANG!!
<NEXT TIME, I WILL ARRANGE FOR DINNER AT A MUCH NICER PLACE, JUNKO-CHAN!>
<NEXT TIME, HUH?>
<TILL THEN, A LITTLE SOMETHING EXTRA? JUST FOR YOU.>
GHEEE!!
S...S... SENSEI!!
SENSEI?

SENSEI...
LARGO-SENSEI!
TEACHER LARGO!!!
PLEASE...
PLEASE DON'T TELL MY PARENTS. LARGO-SENSEI.
PLEASE...
WHY WOULD I SPEAK TO YOUR PARENTS?
BECAUSE... YOU'RE MY TEACHER.
PLEASE DON'T TELL THEM! MY MOM, SHE'D... SHE'D...
I AM NO ONE'S TEACHER.
GO BACK TO YOUR GAME.

<BUT... YOU... ARE IN THE STORE ALL THE TIME.>
<YOU'VE BOUGHT LOTS OF MANGA, ANIME, CDS...>
<YOU'VE TRIED ON COSPLAY OUTFITS AND-->
<WHY SHOULD IT MATTER TO YOU WHAT I BUY?!?>
<WHAT ARE YOU, MY MOTHER?!?>
<NO...>
<OBVIOUSLY.>
<HAYASAKA-SAN...>
<YOU'RE THE ONE WHO'S FAMOUS, AND PRETTY, AND TALENTED AND ALL THE THINGS I'LL NEVER BE.>
<YOU ALWAYS HAVE TO BE THE IMPORTANT ONE, DON'T YOU?>
<IF YOU ARE SO FAMOUS, WHY DO YOU WORK HERE, ANYWAY?>
<HEY! THAT'S ENOUGH. LEAVE HER ALONE.>

<SHE'S HAD A ROUGH WEEK, LEAVE HER ALONE.>
<M...MISS PERFECT STARTED IT! I WAS JUST SITTING HERE!!>
<"MISS PERFECT...">
<IF I REALLY WAS "MISS PERFECT", YOUR PARENTS WOULDN'T HAVE WORRIED ABOUT THE NEGATIVE IMPACT I MIGHT HAVE HAD ON YOU.>
<SO WORRIED THAT THEY EVEN PREVENTED ME FROM MEETING YOU.>
<HUH?>
<YOUR DAD IS INSPECTOR SONODA WITH THE TOKYO POLICE CATACLYSM DIVISION, CORRECT?>
<T... TOKYO POLICE??>
<UH... YES. HOW DID YOU-->
<I WAS TOLD THAT YOUR PARENTS DIDN'T WANT YOU EXPOSED TO THE KIND OF WORK I DID.>
<BUT HERE YOU ARE AS INTO MANGA, ANIME AND MUSIC AS ANY GIRL YOUR AGE.>
<THAT'S... GOOD. I'M GLAD.>
<I ALWAYS WORRIED THAT YOUR PARENTS WERE BEING OVERLY PROTECTIVE.>
<IT'S GOOD TO KNOW THAT IT WASN'T MY WORK IN ANIME THAT WAS THE PROBLEM...>
<IT WAS ME.>
<HAYA-SAKA-SAMA? CAN YOU SIGN MY DVD BOX SET?>
<SURE. WHAT'S YOUR NAME?>

¥ ARCADE
WHOSH! SCREEECH!
BING BING BING!!
HWEEE! CHING!
WHOOM!
TWANG!
SKISH!!
TING TING TING!!
WHAM!
DANCEDAN WHEEE!
WHUP! WHUP! SCREEEECH!
FZZZT! WHOOM!!!
ZZZOOOM!!
BAM! BAM!!
PLEASE TELL ME YOU AREN'T JUST LYING THERE TO TRY AND PEEK UP GIRLS' SKIRTS.
BEEP! BEEP!
SCREEEECH! CRASH!!
FWOOM!!
BING BING! BING!!
VROOM! VROOM!

YOU REEK OF BOOZE. ARE YOU OK?
DID THE SCHOOL COME TO ITS SENSES AND FIRE YOU?
COME ON, LET'S GET YOU SOME COFFEE.
LET GO OF ME.
I WILL STAND ON MY OWN.
I WAS ONLY TRYING TO HELP. YOU DON'T HAVE TO BE A JERK ABOUT IT.
SO, WHAT HAPPENED TO "GREAT TEACHER LARGO?"
"GREAT TEACHER LARGO" WOULDN'T LET A SIMPLE THING LIKE GETTING FIRED STOP HIM FROM TEACHING HIS GAR-BAGE.
YOU QUIT, DIDN'T YOU?
I CHOSE NOT TO PLAY.
SAME THING.

THE STUDENTS THINK OF YOU AS SOME KIND OF HERO, PROBABLY BECAUSE YOU SAVE THEM FROM ACTUALLY LEARNING ANY-THING.
HOW ARE THEY GOING TO FEEL WHEN THEY FIND OUT "GREAT TEACHER LARGO" QUIT?
SENSEI?
SENSEI, WAIT!
MGS
4
KONAMI
SENSEI?
OHHHH! WHO'S THAT? IS HE FROM A GAME?
HE'S *CUTE!!*
SENSEI?

<HUH, THIS ONE IS REALLY NICE TOO.>
<Y'KNOW...>
<YOU'RE REALLY GOOD! HOW LONG HAVE YOU BEEN DRAWING?>
<THERE ARE SOME WEIRD PROPORTIONS HERE AND THERE, BUT OVERALL...>
<YOU'RE GOOD! I DON'T KNOW WHAT I CAN TEACH YOU.>
<YOU'RE BETTER THAN I AM.>
<NO I'M NOT. EVERYTHING IN HERE IS JUST COPIES OF OTHER PEOPLE'S DRAWINGS.>
<NONE OF THEM ARE MINE.>
<BUT YOU DREW THEM, RIGHT? FREEHAND? TRACED?>
<FREE-HAND.>
<THAT'S GOOD! THAT'S HOW YOU LEARN! I'M SURE IF YOU TRIED-->
<NO, I CAN COPY. THAT'S ALL I CAN DO.>
FLIP
<WHENEVER I TRY TO DRAW SOMETHING WITHOUT COPYING AN EXISTING DRAWING, IT LOOKS TERRIBLE.>
<BORING, DULL, LIFELESS, POINTLESS.>
<IT MAKES ME SICK TO LOOK AT THEM.>
<I ALWAYS TEAR THEM OUT AND THROW THEM AWAY.>
<I WANT TO LEARN HOW TO DRAW WHAT I FEEL INSIDE, TO PUT REAL FEELINGS INTO THEM, LIKE YOU DO.>
<HUH? LIKE I WHAT?>
<DRAW FEELINGS.>
<YOU KNOW, THOSE FRAGILE THINGS THAT GET HURT A LOT?>
FLIP FLIP

<FEELINGS? BUT I DON'T-->
<YES YOU DO. HERE. LOOK.>
<THIS IS A COPY I MADE OF ONE OF YOUR DRAWINGS.
<YOU CAN FEEL HER SADNESS, EVEN IN MY COPY.>
<UHH... THAT'S GOOD! YOUR DRAWING HAS LOTS OF FEELING IN IT!>
<NO, THE FEELING IN IT COMES FROM YOU. IT'S NOT MY "FEELING" AT ALL.>
<ALL OF YOUR DRAWINGS HAVE A DEEP KIND OF SADNESS IN THEM, SOMETHING THAT COMES FROM YOU.>
<I WANT YOU TO SHOW ME HOW YOU DO IT.>
<UH... IT'S THE... CHARACTERS THAT ARE SAD, NOT ME.>
<THEY AREN'T... MY FEELINGS.>
<SO UH...>
<WHEN YOU DRAW YOUR GIRL-FRIEND...>
<DO YOU DRAW HER LOOKING SAD?>

<UH...>
<OH, SHE'S NOT MY GIRLFRIEND.>
<SHE'S...>
<A FRIEND.>
<I MEAN...>
<I WISH SHE WAS MY GIRL-FRIEND.>
<NOTHING WOULD MAKE ME HAPPIER.>
<IT'S NICE TO FANTASIZE ABOUT.>
<BUT I REALLY SHOULDN'T GET MY HOPES...>
<IT'S A SILLY QUESTION ANYWAY.>
<I CAN'T DRAW REAL PEOPLE. JUST CHARACTERS.>
<IF I TRIED TO DRAW HER I'M SURE IT WOULD **MAKE** HER SAD.>
<AND I WOULDN'T WANT THAT.>
CLICK
CLICK
<OK! I THINK I SHOULD STOP WASTING YOUR TIME AND TRY TO TEACH YOU SOME-THING, SONODA-SAN.>
<WHY DON'T YOU DRAW ME SOME-THING AND LET'S SEE IF I CAN HELP YOU GET SOME "FEELING" INTO IT.>

LOOK, SENSEI, MAYBE ENGLISH JUST ISN'T YOUR SUBJECT!
NO MORE HEROES...
I MEAN, HONESTLY, YOU ARE NOT VERY GOOD AT TEACHING ENGLISH.
BUT THAT DOESN'T MEAN...
...YOU ARE A BAD TEACHER.
Punished Pinion
Punished Pinion
HERE, LET ME SHOW YOU SOME-THING.
-FUMP!-
Punished Pinion
I'VE NEVER PLAYED THESE KINDS OF GAMES BEFORE.
IN FACT, I NEVER WANTED TO.
BUT YOU MADE ME TRY.
YOU WOULDN'T LET ME GIVE UP.
A GOOD TEACHER NEVER LETS YOU GIVE UP.

WHY WON'T YOU FIGHT?!
krick
YOU JUST GONNA STAND THERE AND LET ME KICK THE CRAP OUT OF YOU?
YOU THINK I'M NOT WORTH TAKING ON?
COME'ON, FIGHT!
FIGHT!!
FEH.
LET'S JUST GET THIS OVER WITH.
SHUFF

WHUD!
HUFF
/\/\3G4 \/\/RLD ROX4G3, DOOD. M3G4.
I do not think she will be getting up after that one.
OK SENSEI, LET'S TRY THAT AGAIN! I THINK I KNOW WHAT I DID WRONG!
53|\|531? DI5 S3X4 LIL .JP CHIXOR J00 57|_|D3|\|7?
Punished Pinion
Is this young lady one of your pupils?
YES.
T3H \/\/I|\| DOOD.
I am impressed.
TAT TATTAT
H3Y B4B3, J00 GOTZ 2 M4K3 W/632I46S FOR M4X B33TZ.
<WHAT??>
Young lady, your prowess is admirable, but I think you should channel your ki into a killing strike. You could own his butt hardcore.

2 L8. P2 P\/\/|\|Z3D JOO.
<WHAT?>
Ah, you did not act quickly enough. Now the advantage is his.
TAK TAK TAK TAK
WH3N P2 IN /\/\155 FR4/\/\3, M4K3 W/THROW FRC 5S5SJCJ.KJ-.SJCJ.H236K6-23K214K.
<WHY ARE YOU TALKING TO ME??>
TAK TAK TAK
When he stops hitting you, you should turn and hit him with a powerful move.
OHH... M4D 6K [0/\/\B0. SW33T.
<WAHH??? NOOOO!!>
Nevermind. you are toast.
<NOO! DAMNIT! NO, NO, NO, NO!!>
Punished Pinion
TAK TAK TAK TAK TAK TAK TAKTAK TAK TAK TAKTAK
WHACK!
CRASH
CHIKAN!!

NANI YATTENNO?? CHOU HENTAI!!
[|-||_|_. GRRL, [|-||_|_! 3Y3 /=...
-URK-
My apologies, young lady, I did not mean to -- oh dear.
EH?
D4... D4 P4I|\|...!
I think I feel pain in my chest.
UWAH! NA... NANI?
B4D... P4IN... N33D... PI|_|_Z...
Yes, it is pain. I probably should take my medication.
UH33HH...
-THUD-
EHHH? S... SENSEI! HELP!!
No, i think I will fall down instead.
SENSEI! IS HE OK? WHAT IS HE SAYING?
HE NEEDS TO TAKE HIS PILLS. HE WILL BE FINE.
DUD3... DA... P4I|\|...
WHY DID YOU HIT HIM AND CALL HIM "CHICKEN"?
HE WAS TRYING TO HELP YOU.
B... BECAUSE HE IS ONE!!
GULP
THAT DOESN'T GIVE HIM THE RIGHT TO TAKE ADVANTAGE OF ME!!
|_|G|-|...
WHY ARE YOU CONCERNED ABOUT HIM?
WO4H... H3DZ... SPINNZ...
WELL... I... I DON'T WANT HIM TO DIE, I JUST--
SPO7S...
EH? WHAT?
PINK... LIL' POKA... DOTS...
i see spots, lots of little, floating spots before my eyes...
DIE!!!
HM.
WHAK!
UW4H!
Ow.

I THINK YOU DAMAGED HIM.
W04H... 3VRY7NG MOOVIN', SHPINNIN...
WELL, IT'S HIS OWN FAULT FOR LOOKING UP MY--
<WAIT... I'M NOT WEARING PINK POLKA DOTS TODAY, I'M WEARING THE GREEN STRIPED...>
<OH.>
DO ALL WOMEN FEEL THREATENED WHEN YOU TRY TO HELP THEM?
DO THEY FEEL IT IS A COWARDLY ATTEMPT TO LEARN THEIR WEAKNESSES AND TAKE ADVANTAGE OF THEM?
WELL, NO, NOT IF YOU DO IT WITH RESPECT AND GOOD INTENTIONS.
FOR EXAMPLE, TRYING TO LOOK UP A GIRL'S SKIRT DOESN'T SAY "GOOD INTENTIONS" TO ANY GIRL.
INTER-ESTING.
WHAT ABOUT TRYING TO TEACH ONE SOMETHING DIFFICULT?
THAT'S OK AS LONG AS YOU AREN'T JUST TRYING TO SHOW OFF. NOTHING IS MORE ANNOYING THAN SOME GUY WHO THINKS HE KNOWS EVERY-THING.
EVEN IF HE HAS M4D SKILLZ?
WHAT?

<OK, DON'T CROWD. I CAN ONLY DO ONE AT A TIME.>
<ARE YOU GONNA DO A COMEBACK CONCERT??>
<CAN YOU SIGN A BUNCH OF THINGS FOR MY CLUB?>
<AH...>
<DO YOU THINK SHE'D SIGN MY DOLLFIE'S BLOOMERS?>
<HEY, YOU GOT YOUR AUTOGRAPH! MOVE!>
<HAYASAKA-SAMA!>
<HAYASAKA-SAMA!>
<NO! I STILL WANT TO LOOK AT HER!>
<UWAEEH...>
<THIS ISN'T COMING OUT AT ALL!>
<THE EYES ARE NOT QUITE RIGHT FOR THE EXPRESSION YOU SEEM TO BE GOING FOR.>
<NEVER BE AFRAID TO ERASE AND REDRAW THINGS. ADDING DETAIL TO EYES THAT ARE THE WRONG SHAPE OR LOCATED WRONG ON THE FACE WON'T MAKE THEM WORK.>
<THE HUMAN FACE HAS ITS OWN, SUBTLE LANGUAGE FOR COMMUNICATING EMOTION, AND IT'S A LANGUAGE WE ALL UNDERSTAND. WE ARE ALL VERY SENSITIVE TO IT.>
<PEOPLE WILL NOTICE EVEN THE MOST SUBTLE CHANGES IN A PERSON'S FACE, EVEN IF THAT PERSON IS A DRAWING...>
<SEE?>
<IS SHE... CRYING?>
<NO, BUT WE CAN MAKE HER CRY IF YOU WANT TO. IT'S PRETTY EASY.>

<SONODA-SAN? WHAT ARE YOU-->
<THAT GIRL IS CRYING!>
<WHAT DO WE DO??>
-SNFF- HFF HNN -SNIFF-
<UHH...>
<TRY ERASING THOSE EYES AND DRAWING THEM AGAIN.>
<I'LL... BE BACK IN A MINUTE.>
<UHM...>
<TOHYA-SAN?>
-SNFF- UNNNNNN...HFF -SNIFF-
<ARE YOU... OK? DID SOME-THING-->
-SNIFF- <H-HOW C-CAN YOU ASK M-M-ME THAT?> -SNIFF-
<AFTER WHAT Y-Y-YOU D-DID TO ME L-LAST NIGHT... -SNIFF- WHAT YOU M-M-MADE M-M-ME ENDURE...>
<WEH?>
<YOU'RE HORRIBLE!!>
<YOU'RE THE WORST!!>

~SNIFF~
HNHN HNNNNN
~SIFF~
<AH... UH...>
<TOHYA-SAN, I DIDN'T MEAN TO... I DIDN'T WANT YOU TO...>
HUN HUN HNNNNNN
~SNIFF~
<UH...>
HNNNNNN NNN HN
<I THINK THAT GUY IS MAKING HER CRY.>
<DO YOU THINK HE'S BREAKING UP WITH HER?>
<CAN YOU SIGN THIS FOR MY SISTER, HAYASAKA-SAN?>
<I'D NEVER MAKE HAYASAKA-SAN CRY!>
<WAI! A FATE/HOLLOW ATARAXIA ARTBOOK!>
<OH COME ON! THOSE ARE THE FAKEST-->
~SNIFF~
HNHN HNNNNN
~SIFF~
CRASH!
<MIHO-CHAN!!>
THUD!
<UWAH!!>
<OW!>
<UYAAH!!>
<OOF!>
<NO, NO!! DON'T HURT ME!!>
<HER BREASTS RUBBED UP AGAINST ME!!>
<AHHHGH!>
<OOF!>
<I'M SORRY, TOHYA-SAN, I'M SORRY! I NEVER MEANT TO... TO...>
<DID YOU SEE HER TOSS THOSE GUYS OUT OF HER WAY??>
<I THINK I'M IN LOVE!>
<PIRO-SAN!! WHAT DID YOU SAY TO HER?!?>
<THAT IS THE MOST AWESOME PINK HAIR I'VE EVER SEEN.>
WAH!
<...WOW.>

<I DIDN'T SAY ANY-THING!!>
<AND...WHY IS YOUR HAIR PINK??>
<I CAN'T BELIEVE YOU ARE FALLING FOR THIS.>
<SHE WANTED TO APOLOGIZE TO YOU, PIRO-KUN. DON'T YELL AT HER!>
<BUT I DIDN'T SAY ANYTHING!! SHE JUST STARTED CRYING!!>
<OH PLEASE! SHE'S TOTALLY FAKING IT!>
WHAT HAS THAT IDIOT GOTTEN HIMSELF INTO NOW...
<UHM, I NEED TO TAKE A QUICK BREAK, OK?>
<HAYASAKA-SAN!!>
<CAN YOU SIGN THIS FOR ME FIRST?>
<CAN I GET A PICTURE WITH YOU, HAYASAKA-SAN?>
<I'VE BEEN WAITING IN LINE FOR-EVER!>
<NOOO! DON'T GO!>
NEED SOME HELP?
A MOST PERSPICACIOUS GIRL...
<A WHAT?>
HUH?
THE SPECTACLE MAY BE... DELIBERATE.
BUT MY PERTURBATION IS UNFEIGNED.
I COULD SCARE THEM AWAY FOR YOU.
SHOOT A FEW OF THEM IN THE HEAD.
I COULD RIP YOUR HEAD OFF AND THROW IT AT THEM.
OK, I'M GAME.

MAKE SURE YOU GET A GOOD SPIN ON IT. MAKES FOR A BETTER SPRAY PATTERN.
WOULDN'T WANT TO WASTE MY HEAD ON A LAME TOSS.
WHAT'S THE MATTER? NOT AFRAID OF A LITTLE BLOOD, ARE YOU?
<WHAT A BASTARD!>
<HE'S MAKING HER CRY!>
<POOR THING!!>
<MIHO-CHAN?>
SP... SPECTACLE??
<WHAT A JERK!>
<ARE YOU OPEN? I'D LIKE TO GET THESE.>
<UWAE?>
<HAYASAKA-SAMA!!>
<UHM... PLEASE, DON'T CROWD! JUST ONE MORE AND THEN I REALLY HAVE TO-->
NO... YOU AREN'T AFRAID OF VIOLENCE. IN FACT, YOU ARE INFAMOUS FOR IT.
YET EVEN YOU ARE POWERLESS WHEN IT COMES TO THE FRAGILITY OF HOW PEOPLE PERCEIVE YOU.
Y'KNOW... I WONDER HOW WELL YOUR FRIEND WILL HANDLE THINGS THE FIRST TIME SHE HAS TO DEAL WITH HER "IMAGE."
I CERTAINLY HOPE SHE DOESN'T GET... HURT OR ANYTHING.
FANS CAN BE SO... UNPREDICTABLE.
<"CAN'T WAIT TO SEE YOU AT WORK TONIGHT.">
<WHO IN THE WORLD SENT THIS?>

CAREFUL...
FWISH
YOUR SMILE IS SLIPPING.
WORRIED ABOUT YOUR FRIEND?
THAT'S SO SWEET.
TELL YOU WHAT...
IF YOU JOIN US AT SEGA, NOT ONLY WILL WE PROVIDE YOU WITH SUPERIOR PROTECTION AND PEACE OF MIND,
BUT AS A PROFESSIONAL COURTESY I'LL EXTEND THAT SAME LEVEL OF PROTECTION TO YOUR FRIEND.
IT IS LOOKING LIKE SHE'S GOING TO NEED IT.
SO THINK ABOUT IT.

ARE YOU TELLING ME THIS IS ALL SOME KIND OF ACT?
<DO YOU HAVE THE POWDER BLUE VERSION OF THIS FIGURE?>
<I'M SORRY, I DON'T-->
<AH!>
<PIRO-KUN, PLEASE DON'T YELL AT HER!>
<I'M NOT YELLING!>
-breeeee- -breeeee-
<YES YOU ARE!>
<BUT I... SHE'S THE ONE WHO... I...>
<WHY ARE YOU BEING SO MEAN, PIRO-KUN?>
<WHAT?? I'M NOT DOING ANYTHING!! SHE'S THE ONE WHO, WHO...>
breeeee-
<PIRO-SAN?>
<YES?>
<YOUR PHONE.>
<IT'S THAT CALL YOU'VE BEEN WAITING FOR ALL MORNING.>
<EH?>
<YOUR PHONE.>
<AND THIS CUSTOMER HAS A QUESTION.>
<UH...>
<EXCUSE ME! I'LL BE WITH YOU IN A MOMENT!>
<NO PROBLEM.>
-breeeee- -breeeee-

<I'LL BE WITH YOU IN ONE SECOND, SIR.>
<I JUST NEED TO TAKE THIS CALL.>
<HELLO? KIMI-->
<HI! DID EVERYTHING GO OK?>
<A WHAT? A TEXT MES-SAGE?>
<NO, I DIDN'T.>
<YOU DON'T KNOW WHO IT'S FROM?>
<WHAT DID IT SAY?>
<"CAN'T WAIT TO SEE YOU AT WORK TONIGHT?">
<KIMIKO-SAN! ARE YOU REALLY WORKING TONIGHT??>
<UHM, YES. I USUALLY WORK SUNDAYS 'TILL CLOSE.>
<YOU CAN'T GO IN TONIGHT! CALL IN SICK!!>
<UWEH? WHY?>
<DO... DO YOU THINK... SOMEONE FOUND OUT WHERE I WORK?>
<YES, AND THEY TOLD EVERYONE ELSE!!>
<THEY KNOW THAT NANASAWA KIMIKO WORKS AT ANNA MILLER'S AND THEY ARE ALL GOING THERE TONIGHT TO SEE HER!!>
<I CAN'T WAIT TO SEE NANASAWA-SAN IN HER WAITRESS OUTFIT.>
<I HOPE SHE LETS ME TAKE SOME PICTURES.>
<I'M GOING STRAIGHT THERE AFTER THIS, I HEAR THERE'S ALREADY A BIG LINE TO GET IN!>

<SO, UHM...>
<ARE YOU GUYS SURE SHE WON'T BE... NERVOUS ABOUT SO MANY FANS SURPRISING HER AT WORK TONIGHT?>
<ARE YOU KIDDING? SHE'S AN ANGEL! IT'LL MAKE HER HAPPY!>
<YEAH! LAST NIGHT SHE CHASED DOWN SOME POOR LONELY OTAKU WHO WAS GOING TO JUMP IN FRONT OF A TRAIN AND SAVED HIS LIFE!>
<A WHAT?? IS THAT WHAT YOU ALL THINK-->
<OH! DID YOU SEE THAT UPSKIRT SHOT SOMEONE MANAGED TO GET OF HER WHEN SHE WAS CHASING HIM?>
<YEAH! SHE'S WEARING BLACK STOCKINGS, BUT YOU CAN TELL...>
<THEY'RE WHITE. PRISTINE, ANGELIC WHITE.>
<I'VE ANALYZED THE PICTURE IN PHOTOSHOP, AND I THINK THERE'S A PINK BOW IN FRONT.>
<REALLY?>
<THE PIC WAS TAKEN WITH ONE OF THOSE NEW 8 MEGAPIXEL PHONES...>
<IS THAT WHY IT'S SO CLEAR?>
<D... DID YOU HEAR ANY OF THAT??>
<KIMIKO-SAN?>
<HELLO?>

<KIMIKO-SAN?>
<HELLO??>
<KIMIKO-SAN!!>
HIS ASTONISHING INEPTITUDE IS BEWILDERING, DON'T YOU THINK?
<EH? WHAT?>
DAMNIT! I LOST HER!
REDIAL, REDIAL...
<YOU REALLY ARE A STUPID LITTLE GIRL, AREN'T YOU?>
<YOU THINK I AM BLIND TO YOUR LITTLE TRICKS?>
<WHAT?>
<NA-- KIMIKO-SAN! WHAT HAPPENED? ARE YOU-->
<NO, THAT'S OK, DON'T-->
<WHAT?>
<YOU THINK I DON'T KNOW WHAT YOU'D DO TO STEAL HIS HEART?>
<OH, I KNOW. I KNOW WHAT YOU'D DO.>
<BUT ARE YOU SURE YOU WANT IT THAT BADLY, SONODA-SAN?>
<IT'S A SLIMY, SLIPPERY THING.>

<DID...>
<DID SOME-ONE REALLY...>
<TAKE A PICTURE OF...?>
<I... I THINK SO.>
<WHY WOULD... SOMEONE DO THAT?>
<I... I DON'T... LOOK, NANA-- ER, KIMIKO-SAN, YOU CAN'T GO INTO WORK TONIGHT! IT'S TOO DANGEROUS!>
<WHAT'S THAT SUPPOSED TO MEAN?!?>
<YOU HEARD ME. A LITTLE GIRL LIKE YOU IS JUST A MINI-GAME.>
<SIMPLE, EASILY WON, AND ONLY MILDLY AMUSING. YOU CAN HARDLY EXPECT HIM TO STAY INTERESTED FOR VERY LONG.>
<I AM N-- STOP IT, TOHYA, STOP IT RIGHT NOW!!>
<OH, AM I HURTING YOUR FEELINGS?>
<SHUT UP! SHUT UP!!>
<MIHO-CHAN!!>
OH, ONE LAST THING.
THERE'S A COMPROMISING PHOTOGRAPH OF YOUR FRIEND LOOSE IN THE WILD.
THE FIRST THING I'D DO FOR HER IS ELIMINATE ALL TRACES THAT THE PHOTO EVER EXISTED.
IT IS A SERVICE FEW ORGANIZATIONS CAN OFFER, AND REQUIRES SOME EXTREME MEASURES TO ACCOMPLISH.
SHFFFF!
BUT YOU KNOW ALL THAT.
AND JUST HOW... VALUABLE THE SERVICE CAN BE.
WRUMP!
CRASH!
<AIEEE!!!>
<LOOK OUT!!>
<UWAH!!>
<BUT PIRO-SAN, I'M SCHEDULED TO WORK TONIGHT, I HAVE TO GO IN!>
<PIRO-SAN?>
<HELLO? DID SOMETHING HAPPEN? PIRO-SAN??>

VRRRM!!
VRMMM...
MISTER MUFFIN
I CAN EMPTY THE STORE IN THREE MINUTES AND TWENTY SECONDS.
IF YOU WANT ME TO.

<PIRO-SAN? WHAT'S WRONG? WHAT WAS THAT NOISE?>
<IS EVERY-THING OK?>
DON'T... HURT ANYONE.
-NOD-
<YES! YES! EVERYTHING IS FINE!>
<NOTHING TO WORRY ABOUT! NOTHING AT ALL!>

<MUFFINS!?>
<KYAAAH!>
<WHAT'S HE DOING??>
<HELP!>
<RUN FOR IT!!>
<AIEEE!!>
<CRAZY FAN ON A SCOOTER!!>
<SO, YOU'LL CALL IN SICK TONIGHT, RIGHT?>
<BUT PIRO-SAN... IT'S NOT THE RIGHT THING TO DO!>
<WHAT? WHY?>
<WAHH!>
<RUN AWAY!!>
<RUN AWAY!!>
<LOOK OUT!!>
<HERE! KEEP THE CHANGE!!>
<SAVE ME!!>
<RUN AWAY!!>
<BUT I DIDN'T GET MY DVD SIGNED!!>
<YOU CAN JUST COME BACK TOMORROW!>
<THEY DON'T MEAN ANY HARM, PIRO-SAN, I... I KNOW THAT.>
<IF I RUN AWAY FROM THEM I'M NO BETTER THAN ALL THE OTHERS.>
<WH... WHAT ARE YOU DOING!?!!>

RRRR!
RRRRRR!
<BUT KIMIKO-SAN...>
<I DON'T WANT TO BE HIDDEN AWAY FROM PEOPLE WHO CARE ABOUT ME, PIRO-SAN.>
<EEK!!>
<RUN AWAY!>
<RUN AWAY!>
RRRR!
<LET GO OF ME!!>
<LET GO OF ME!!>
<I DON'T WANT TO BE JUST AN OBJECT TO THEM. IF I DON'T GO, IF I RUN AWAY, IF I DON'T LIVE MY LIFE... THAT'S WHAT I'LL BECOME.>
<UWEH?>
<WAHHH!>
<I'M SORRY, I'M SORRY, I'M SORRY!!>
RRRRN!
-fwip!
<TOHYA!!>
<I'M SORRY!!>

<PIRO-SAN?>
<WHAT WAS THAT NOISE? WHAT'S GOING ON THERE?>
<HELLO?? PIRO-SAN!>
<I THINK...>
<SOMEONE GOT HURT.>
<I'LL CALL YOU BACK.>
<PING!! WHAT HAPPENED??>
<I HEARD A YELL AND THEN-->
WHAT THE...

<SOME-ONE GOT HURT?>
<I HOPE IT'S NOT SERIOUS.>
<WAIT...>
<IF ERIKA HAD OVER-HEARD WHAT THOSE FAN-BOYS WERE SAYING...>
<SHE WOULDN'T-->
<NANA-SAWA-SAN!>
<WHAT ARE YOU DOIN' OUT HERE? DID MATSUI TOSS YOU OUT ON YOUR BUTT?>
<CH...CH... CHIBA-SAN!!>
<HEY.>
AO:1
<SO THESE ARE THE LOCKART OFFICES, HUH? I'VE NEVER ACTUALLY BEEN-->
<I'M... I'M SORRY, CHIBA-SAN! I'M VERY, VERY SORRY ABOUT THE THINGS I SAID TO YOU LAST NIGHT!!>
<WOAH, NANASAWA-SAN, DON'T.>
<I'M THE ONE WHO NEEDS TO APOLOGIZE.>
<IN FACT, THAT'S WHY I CAME DOWN HERE TO SEE YOU.>
<I WANTED TO APOLOGIZE FOR SOME OF THE THINGS I SAID WHEN WE MET. I BELIEVE I MAY HAVE MADE YOU FEEL UNCOMFORTABLE.>
<I'M SORRY.>

WAHHH!!
LARGO!
STOP!
THAT'S GOOD ENOUGH!
THUMP
<WHAT HAPPENED?>
<I... I...>
<T... TOHYA WAS... FALLING AND...>
<FALLING?>
<SHE WAS GONNA GET HURT...>
<AND I... I...>
I HAVE NOT CLEARED THE INFESTATION ON THE UPPER LEVELS YET.
IT CAN WAIT.
VRRM...*
WAIT... YOU WERE GOING TO DRIVE THIS THING UPSTAIRS?
IT CLEARED DOM AND THOSE TABLES, I THINK IT COULD MAKE IT!
<UWAH! MY ANKLE!>
<SONODA-SAN!>
SHFFFFF!
<WHAT THE...>
<YUKI?>

<DAD?>
<D... DAD?>
<WHAT'S GOING ON HERE?>
<NOTHING! I JUST STUMBLED AND-->
<UWAH!!!>
<WHAT ARE YOU DOING IN HERE?!?>
<SHOPPING.>
<THIS STORE CARRIES A LOT OF FUN AND INTERESTING GAMES.>
<Y... YOU KNOW TOHYA-SAN, DAD?>
<MASA-MICHI!>
<ERIKA...>
<YUKI.>
<HOME.>
<NOW.>

<WHAT?? GO HOME?? WHY?>
<MASAMICHI, WAIT. SHE DIDN'T DO ANYTHING WRONG.>
<SHE DIDN'T KNOW I WORKED HERE! I DIDN'T EVEN KNOW WHO SHE-->
<NO!! ERIKA! STAY AWAY FROM HER!!>
<MASAMICHI...>
<I'D NEVER DO ANYTHING TO HURT YOUR DAUGHTER. PLEASE DON'T BE LIKE THIS.>
<DAD?>
<I BELIEVE HE IS REFERRING TO ME.>
<I THINK HE'S WORRIED THAT I MIGHT BITE YOU.>
<WHAT?>
<THE INSPECTOR THINKS I'M DANGER-OUS.>
<WHY? ROUTINE VIOLATIONS OF THE DRESS CODE?>
<NO.>
<THIS GIRL CAUSED...>
<SOME REAL PROBLEMS...>
<BACK THEN.>
<BACK THEN?>
<I WAS ONCE A BIG FAN OF YOURS.>
<A FAN OF YOUR FANS, TO BE MORE PRECISE.>

<MY FANS?>
<YOUR FANS BECAME VERY EMOTIONAL WHEN YOU LEFT THEM THE WAY YOU DID, HAYASAKA-SAN.>
WHAT ARE THEY SAYING?
I DON'T KNOW.
TRANS-LATE.
OK.
<IT WAS OVERWHELMING. A VAST MULTITUDE... UNHAPPY, SAD, UPSET.>
<YOU TOOK ADVANTAGE OF A VERY, VERY BAD SITUATION.>
<PERHAPS. BUT IN THE END IT DIDN'T WORK OUT VERY WELL FOR ME, DID IT?>
<NO...>
<NO IT DIDN'T.>
<MASAMICHI, WHAT DID THIS GIRL DO?>
<RELAX, INSPECTOR. I HAVE NO DESIRE TO LIVE THROUGH SUCH AN EXPERIENCE AGAIN.>
<SO, EXACTLY HOW LONG HAVE YOU BEEN... UP?>
<A WHILE. YOU'VE SEEN ME YOURSELF SEVERAL TIMES SINCE I WAS RELEASED FROM THE HOSPITAL.>
<WHAT??>
<OH COME NOW, INSPECTOR. YOU KNOW FULL WELL THAT PEOPLE OFTEN DON'T SEE WHAT IS RIGHT IN FRONT OF THEM IF THEY DON'T EXPECT IT TO BE THERE.>
<ESPECIALLY IF IT DOESN'T MATCH WHAT THEY EXPECT TO SEE.>
<A QUIET SCHOOL GIRL WITH HAIR HACKED MERCILESSLY SHORT.>
<A BITTER STORE CLERK WITH HER LONG HAIR UP.>
<A BLISSFUL MOTHER OF TWO WITH HERS DOWN.>
<THAT'S ENOUGH.>

<YUKI! I TOLD YOU TO GO HOME!!>
<BUT...>
<EASY, INSPECTOR.>
<I'M DONE SHOPPING. I'LL BE GOING NOW.>
<I'VE FOUND ENOUGH GAMES TO KEEP ME DISTRACTED FOR QUITE SOME TIME.>
<I'VE EVEN FOUND A NEW ONE TO PLAY.>
<WHAT KIND OF GAMES?>
<WHY? DO YOU THINK **SHE** MIGHT WANT TO PLAY WITH ME AGAIN?>
<LEAVE HER OUT OF THIS. WHAT ARE YOU UP TO?>
<IT'S REALLY NONE OF YOUR BUSINESS, INSPECTOR.>
<SONODA-SAN.>
<EH? YES?>
<THANK YOU.>
<FOR THE SAVE.>
SHFFFFF!

<WHAT WAS THAT ALL ABOUT?>
<YUKI.>
<GO OUTSIDE AND GET IN THE MECH. I'LL TAKE YOU HOME.>
<WHAT? WHY? WHAT DID-->
<I SAID GET IN THE MECH.>
<BUT-->
<NOW!!>
<MASAMICHI, IF THIS IS ABOUT HER BEING HERE, PLEASE HEAR ME OUT.>
<IF I HAD KNOWN WHO SHE WAS, I WOULD HAVE MADE SURE THAT I NEVER HAD ANY CONTACT WITH HER.>
<I UNDERSTAND AND RESPECT THE FACT THAT YOU AND MEIMI DID NOT WANT ME TO HAVE ANY CONTACT WITH YOUR CHILDREN.>
<"GO HOME, YUKI!" "GET IN THE MECH, YUKI!">
<WHAT'S HE SO MAD ABOUT? I DIDN'T DO ANYTHING WRONG!!>
<ALL I DID WAS...>
<WAS...>
<IF I'VE DONE ANY HARM TO HER AT ALL, I'LL DO WHATEVER IT TAKES TO FIX THE DAMAGE.>
<ERIKA...>
<WHAT IN THE WORLD ARE YOU TALKING ABOUT?>

<WHERE'D YOU GET THE CRAZY IDEA WE DIDN'T WANT YOU NEAR OUR KIDS?>
<HITOSHI SAID... YOU AND MEIMI...>
<HITOSHI SAID? THAT'S ODD...>
<HITOSHI TOLD US THAT YOU HATED CHILDREN.>
WHAT IS BEING SAID?
IT SEEMS TO BE UPSETTING HER.
I'M... NOT REALLY SURE.
SOME KIND OF MISUNDERSTANDING, I THINK.
<HE ASKED US NEVER TO INVITE YOU OVER BECAUSE THE KIDS WOULD MAKE YOU UNCOMFORTABLE.>
<WE'VE NEVER HAD ANY CONCERNS OVER YOU SEEING THEM, ERIKA. NEVER.>
<IN FACT, I ALWAYS WANTED TO SEE YUUJI'S FACE WHEN HE FIGURED OUT THAT HIS UNCLE WAS ENGAGED TO HIS FAVORITE IDOL.>
<HE USED TO HAVE A HUGE POSTER OF YOU IN HIS ROOM, YOU KNOW.>
VRM! VRM
VRRRRRVRM!!
SKREEEK!
VRMVRMVRMVRMVRM
WANT ME TO RUN HIM OVER OR JUST DRIVE HIM OUT?
VRMVRMVRMVRMVRMV

WHAT?
OI. I **AM** A POLICE OFFICER, REMEMBER?
LARGO! NO!
IF I DOUBLE BACK I COULD PICK UP ENOUGH VELOCITY TO V3CTOR HIM THROUGH THE GLASS.
HEY, DON'T MAKE ME GO BAD COP ON YOU.
NO!!
LARGO, PLEASE, DON'T...
IT'S OK.
<OH, ERIKA, YOU MIGHT FIND THIS AMUSING.>
<MEIMI SOMEHOW GOT IT IN HER HEAD THAT YOU WERE DATING THIS WALKING DISASTER.>
<CAN YOU IMAGINE?>
<THE MIND BOGGLES AT WHAT A CATACLYSMIC DISASTER...>
<ERIKA...>
<MY BUDGET...>

<SO WHEN MEIMI SENT ME DOWN HERE TO INVITE **BOTH** OF THEM TO DINNER TOMORROW NIGHT, SHE **WASN'T** JOKING.>
<WOW. ERIKA AND LARGO?>
<I DON'T KNOW IF TOKYO CAN HANDLE THE DAMAGE THOSE TWO ARE CAPABLE OF.>
POLICE
<NO, TOKYO CAN TAKE IT.>
<BUT THAT TOHYA GIRL...>
<THE ONE TIME I ALMOST LOST TOKYO.>
<YUKI? ARE YOU STRAPPED IN?>
<WE NEED TO TALK.>
<YUKI?>
POLICE
<YUKI!!>
<WHAT HAPPENED TO THE DAYS WHERE "GO PLAY IN THE MECH" COULD KEEP THEM HAPPY FOR HOURS?>
POLICE

WHY WOULD YOU AGREE TO LET THIS COP FEED US AT HIS PERSONAL RESIDENCE?
FREE FOOD IS USUALLY T3H WIN, BUT THIS...
SMELLS LIKE A TRAP.
LARGO...
CAN YOU...
HELP PIRO CLEAN UP?
I...
NEED SOME AIR.
SHFFFFF!
YOU'RE STILL HERE?
GO ON. I CAN GET THIS.
IT'S NOT THE WORST MESS YOU'VE EVER MADE.

SHFFFFF!
VRRR
KIMIKO-SAN! I HAVE TO CALL HER BACK!
I HOPE I CAN CHANGE HER MIND ABOUT GOING.
BUT WHAT IF I--
<PING?>
<ARE YOU OK? WHAT'S WRONG?>
<PING?>
SLEEP MODE? NO, THAT LOOK...
SYSTEM CRASH? KERNEL PANIC?
<I ALMOST KILLED MY BEST FRIEND.>
<WHAT?>
<THAT OTHER GIRL...>
<HAD TO RESCUE HER FROM ME.>
<I'M NOT A HEROINE.>
<I'M A...>
<A BAD CHARACTER.>

<IT'S ALL MY FAULT!>
KTHUMP
<MIHO-CHAN... WAS HURTING SO BAD... AFTER WHAT YOU SAID... TO HER.>
<SHE WANTED... TO GIVE UP... TO LET IT ALL GO... TO GO AWAY...>
<BUT I WOULDN'T LET HER! I MADE HER COME HERE! AND... AND...>
<LOOK AT WHAT HAPPENED!!>
<WOAH, PING, CALM DOWN.>
<SHE GOT UPSET...>
<SHE GOT ANGRY...>
<SHE GOT SCARED...>
<SHE GOT HURT...>
<IT'S MY FAULT!>
<I'M A HORRIBLE CHARACTER!!>
<YOU'RE NOT A HORRIBLE CHARACTER, PING.>
<YOU'D ONLY BE HORRIBLE IF YOU **WANTED** TO HURT HER. WE ALL HURT PEOPLE WITHOUT MEANING TO SOME-TIMES.>
<R... REALLY?>
<YES, REALLY. I DO IT ALL THE TIME.>
<BUT... MIHO-CHAN...>
<I'M SURE SHE'LL UNDER-STAND.>
<WAAAAHHHH!!>
<PIRO-KUN!!>
<UH... PING?>

<PIRO-KUN IS A GOOD PERSON. PIRO-KUN DIDN'T WANT TO HURT MIHO-CHAN.>
<UH... OF COURSE NOT.>
<PIRO-KUN DOESN'T WANT TO HURT PING.>
MODE: CONFLICTED
COMFORT DESIRED
GAME DATA ERROR [BAD CRC]
<WHAT? WHY WOULD I WANT TO HURT YOU?>
<PIRO-KUN IS A GOOD PERSON.>
<PIRO-KUN WANTS TO CALL NANASAWA-SAN.>
<HUH? UH... YEAH, I... TOLD HER I'D CALL HER BACK.>
<I HAVE TO TRY TO-->
<PIRO-KUN...>
<DON'T LET NANASAWA-SAN GET HURT...>
<PIRO-KUN.>
<I'M GOING TO GO FIND MIHO-CHAN!>
<BYE BYE, PIRO-KUN!>
<NO, PING, WAIT!!>
IS SHE REALLY OK?
SHE WAS TREMBLING. I COULD FEEL IT...
EVEN WHEN THEY HAVE DIGITAL READOUTS, I CAN'T UNDERSTAND THEM.

<I THINK THAT COVERS MOST OF IT. IT'S A VERY INTENSE SCHEDULE.>
<THINK YOU CAN HANDLE IT?>
<I'LL DO MY BEST.>
<HELLO? NIDERA-SAN? RYOUYA SAYURI HERE.>
<YES, HI! HOW ARE YOU?>
<THE "SIGHT" EVENT ON TUESDAY WILL BE YOUR FIRST PUBLIC APPEARANCE. IT DOESN'T GIVE US A LOT OF TIME TO PREPARE.>
<WE'LL NEED SECURITY, TOO...>
<WHAT ABOUT TONIGHT?>
<TONIGHT?>
<YES, AT THE ANNA MILLER'S IN MEGURO, WHERE I WORK.>
<ISN'T THERE-->
<WHAT?>
<YOU'RE STILL WORKING THAT WAITRESS JOB?>
<YES, I'M SCHEDULED TO-->
<WELL, GET UN-SCHED-ULED.>
<YOU HAVE THEM? GOOD. CAN YOU...>
<BUT I-->
<NANASAWA. 82% OF THE OTAKU CONSUMER MARKET IS FOCUSED ON YOU RIGHT NOW.>
<I THINK CONTINUING TO WORK AS A WAITRESS WOULD BE CERTIFIABLY INSANE.>
<YOU CAN? WONDER-FUL! PLEASE DO!>
<IMAGINE WHAT WOULD HAPPEN IF THEY FOUND OUT WHERE YOU WORKED?>
<TALK ABOUT A NIGHTMARE...>
<NIIDERA-SAN, CAN YOU REPLAY THAT LAST ONE FOR ME?>
<THANKS!>
<NANASAWA, YOUR AGENT IS PLAYING ME TRACKS FROM YOUR DEMO TAPE.>
<I'LL PUT IT ON SPEAKER PHONE.>
<REHHH????>

<THAT'S ONE OF HAYASAKA'S LATER TUNES, ISN'T IT?>
<NOT EVERYONE CAN BELT OUT ONE OF THOSE AND SOUND GOOD DOING IT.>
<THANK YOU, NIIDERA-SAN. IF YOU COULD BRING THOSE OVER AS...>
<GREAT! SEE YOU THEN.>
<I'M IMPRESSED.>
<I HAD NO IDEA YOU COULD SING LIKE THAT, NANA-SAWA.>
<I'VE...>
<HAD SOME TRAINING, AND A FRIEND OF MINE HAS LOTS OF STUDIO EXPERIENCE, SO...>
<I DON'T SEE HER DOING POP MATERIAL, BUT A MOVING BALLAD...>
<LIKE THE ED TRACK FOR THE GOOD ENDING?>
<WHADYA THINK?>
<I THINK UEDA NEEDS TO HEAR HER-->
<NO!! PLEASE!>
<I GET... REALLY EMOTIONAL WHEN I SING.>
<I TEAR UP AND I START CRYING, I... CAN'T STOP IT.>
<I TEAR UP JUST LISTENING TO MUSIC SOME-TIMES! THAT'S WHY I GAVE UP ON SINGING AS A...>
<I CAN DO IT, BUT IT WRECKS ME.>
<UWAH! JUST LOOK AT ME! I CRY JUST THINKING ABOUT IT!!>
<I'M SORRY!> -SNIFF-
<DAMMIT...>
<DO YOU THINK I SHOULD HUG HER?>
<AFTER THIS, THE ONLY GAMES I'M GONNA PRODUCE ARE VIOLENTLY DEPRAVED KICHIKU BLOOD-BATHS.>

<ANOTHER TEXT MESSAGE?>
<HOW DID THEY GET A HOLD OF MY NUMBER?>
<WHAT AM I GONNA DO?>
<THEY SOUND SO EXCITED TO SEE ME.>
<I CAN'T JUST NOT GO.>
<THEY THINK COMING TO SEE ME AT WORK TONIGHT WILL MAKE ME HAPPY.>
<DO THEY ALSO THINK OBSESSING ABOUT PICTURES OF MY UNDERWEAR MAKES ME HAPPY?>
0419
0419
<NO. BAD KIMIKO. DON'T BE LIKE THAT. THEY DON'T MEAN IT.>
0419
<IT'S SO SAD. THEY THINK I'LL BE HAPPY BECAUSE THEY ARE HAPPY.>
<IS THIS WHAT IT'S LIKE TO BE PART OF OTHER PEOPLE'S FANTASIES?>

<DAD'S PROBABLY REALLY MAD AT ME NOW.>
<WHATEVER. HE CAN DEAL WITH IT.>
<OW~ MY ANKLE IS REALLY STARTING TO HURT.>
<WHAT'S WITH HIM ANYWAYS? WHY DOES HE THINK TOHYA IS SOME KIND OF DELINQUENT?>
<SO SHE'S A LITTLE WEIRD. SHE'S NOT A BAD PERSON...>
<I WAS SO SCARED. I'D NEVER BEEN CAUGHT BEFORE.>
<HOW DID THESE GET IN YOUR BAG?>
<I... I... I...>
<OFFICER, WAIT.>
<SHE SAID SHE DID IT BECAUSE SHE WAS A "BAD" GIRL.>
<I PUT THEM IN HER BAG.>
<SHE DIDN'T KNOW. I WAS JUST USING HER.>
<PEOPLE EXPECTED HER TO DO THINGS LIKE THAT, SO IT WAS NO BIG DEAL.>
<SHE SAVED ME.>
<DID I...>
<JUST SAVE HER?>
<WHY DO I HAVE PIRO-SAN'S BOOK-BAG??>
breep! breep!

<IT'S A TEXT MESSAGE...>
<PIRO-SAN, ARE YOU THERE? I REALLY NEED TO TALK TO YOU.>
<KIMIKO>
Docomo
<FROM THAT GIRL.>
<I NEED TO RETURN THESE.>
<I NEVER SHOULD HAVE-->
<YEEEE~!!>
<OWW... MY ANKLE!!>
<SONODA-
<SONODA-SAN?>
<ARE YOU OK? WHAT'S WRONG? DO YOU NEED HELP?>
<Y... YOU'RE TOHYA-SAN'S FRIEND.>
<ARE YOU HURT? CAN YOU STAND?>

<OW!!>
<YOU HAVE A GRADE I SPRAIN OF THE ANTERIOR TALOFIBLULAR LIGAMENT. YOU SHOULDN'T BE WALKING ON IT.>
<WHY DO YOU NEED TO GO BACK TO THE STORE? IT'S A LONG WALK FROM HERE!>
<I...>
<FORGOT SOMETHING, THATS ALL!>
<I'M SORRY I DIDN'T RECOGNIZE YOU, PING-SAN.>
<YOUR... HAIR! IT'S SUCH AN AMAZING COLOR NOW!>
<IT WAS JUST A PALE GREY WHEN I MET YOU THE OTHER DAY.>
<IT WAS?>
<YOU MEAN IT HASN'T ALWAYS BEEN THIS COLOR?>
<I WISH I COULD COLOR MY HAIR. MOM WON'T LET ME.>
<UHM...>
<YOU DIDN'T SEE ME DO ANY-THING...>
<UNUSUAL... EARLIER, IN THE STORE... DID YOU?>
<YOU MEAN LIKE LEAP 4.7 METERS STRAIGHT THROUGH THE AIR AND SAVE MIHO-CHAN FROM GETTING HURT?>
<UWAEEEHH??? YOU SAW THAT???>
<UH HUH! YOU WERE REALLY AMAZING, SONODA-SAN!>

KILL P4K
beep!
POOR LITTLE PLASTIC GIRLIE.
YOU JUST WANDERED OUT OF THE PROTECTIVE RADIUS OF THAT LEVEL 9 EX-IDO
KERCHACK!
IT'S SO SAD. I THINK I'M GONNA CRY.
KER-CHICK!
SHRAPNEL FROM HER EXPLODING HEAD WILL TAKE OUT THE LITTLE GIRL NEXT TO HER.
OH WELL. ENTERTAININGLY ACCEPTABLE COLLATERAL DAMAGE.
BYE BYE, LITTLE GIRLIES.
KILL P4K
FWISH!
IT'S NOT NICE TO BREAK OTHER PEOPLE'S TOYS, YOUNG MAN.

LI'L GRRLI3 GOTZ A DEATH WISH.
YOU THINK?
beep. beep. BEEBEEBEEBEEBEEBEEBEEBEEBEEBEEB *
FWIP!
OMG.
YOU...
YOU'RE...
THE REAL THING.
HEH.
HEH HEH HEH.
HA HAHAHA HAH!!
THE REAL THING!
I... I THINK I FEEL IT...
YES! I CAN!! I'M FEELING...
PH34R!! THIS IS PH34R!
YES!! THAT MUST BE WHAT THIS IS!!!
I NEED BIGGER GUNS!!
DON'T MOVE!! I'LL BE BACK!!

<SO, HOW ARE YOU REALLY HOLDING UP?>
<NO OFFENSE, BUT YOU LOOK LIKE YOU ARE ON THE VERGE OF PANIC.>
<I DO? I'M SORRY.>
<ARE YOU FEELING A LITTLE OVER-WHELMED BY IT ALL?>
<AH!>
BEEHP BEEHP
BEEHP
<NANA-SAWA?>
<YOU'VE BEEN JUMPING AT YOUR PHONE ALL AFTERNOON. WHAT'S THIS GUY MESSAGING YOU ABOUT?>
<GUY? WHAT GUY?>
<I DON'T MEAN TO BE FORWARD, BUT YOU DON'T HAVE TIME FOR RELATIONSHIP ISSUES RIGHT NOW.>
<I KNOW.>
<DON'T WORRY, I CAN HANDLE IT.>

<UWAEHH???>
<HE'S NOT HERE??>
<HE LEFT A WHILE AGO. SAID HE HAD SOME THINGS TO DO.>
<SONODA-SAN? DIDN'T YOU SAY YOU FORGOT SOMETHING HERE?>
<SONODA-SAN?>
breep breep
<YOUR PHONE SURE HAS BEEN BEEPING A LOT, WHY WON'T YOU-->
<REH?>
<THAT'S PIRO-KUN'S PHONE!>
<...i hope you aren't mad at me for going, but i feel i have to. i'm scared, but i can't run away from this. I really wish i could talk to you.>
<please call me?>
<kimiko>
Docomo
<IT...>
<I...>
<I ACCIDENTALLY TOOK IT... EARLIER TODAY.>
<I DIDN'T MEAN TO!>
<THAT GIRL HAS BEEN TRYING TO REACH HIM, SHE SOUNDS UPSET.>
<SHE THINKS HE'S MAD AT HER AND HE DOESN'T WANT TO TALK TO HER...>
<AND IT'S ALL MY FAULT!>
<I'M TOO SCARED TO CALL HER AND TELL HER I TOOK HIS PHONE!>
<I CAN'T LOOK FOR HIM BECAUSE I CAN'T WALK!>
<I DON'T KNOW WHAT TO DO!!>
<DON'T GIVE UP, SONODA-SAN! WE'LL FIND HIM!!>
<WE'LL TAKE THE CITY APART IF WE HAVE TO!>

CHOOSING PATHS AT RANDOM.
AN EXCURSION WITH NO DESTINATION.
WALKIN' OFF T3H W33PIES.
PIRO DOES THIS WHEN HE GETS ALL MOPEY AND LAME.
YOU'RE NOT THE MOST SENSITIVE PERSON IN THE WORLD, ARE YOU.
GIMMIE SOME QUARTERS. I SEE A B33R MACHINE.

WOOT.
SCREECH!
THOSE MACHINES HAD BIG 455 KING SIZ3 CANZ O B334, AND THESE...
LARGO...
JARS OF BOOZ3?
LET ME MAKE SOMETHING CLEAR.
I DON'T NEED YOU.
SO?
I DON'T NEED YOU EITHER.
HERE.
FWIP!

WAP!
IS DRINKING YOUR ANSWER TO EVERYTHING?
NO, NOT EVERY-THING.
OHH!!
IT'S A TOP THAT POPS!!
SW33T!
POP!
IF YOU'RE GONNA DO THE BIG W33PY THING, WAIT TILL I DOWN A FEW OF THESE FIRST.
SHUT UP.
FSHPP!

<AIEEEE!!!>
<SONODA-SAN!!>
<YOU'RE IN TOO MUCH PAIN TO WALK.>
<LET ME CARRY YOU, SONODA -SAN.>
<AHH....>
<PING IS STRONG! I CAN CARRY YOU PIGGY-BACK.>
<N... NO!>
<WHY NOT?>
<BECAUSE! I DON'T WANT TO BE CARRIED LIKE A CHILD!>
<AND...>
<IT'D BE EMBARRASSING...>
<IN THIS SKIRT.>
<QUICK, INTO THIS ALCOVE.>
<EH?>
<LET'S SWAP SKIRTS.>
<UWAEEE??>
<IF WE CAN DO IT IN LESS THAN 5.5 SECONDS, IT WON'T TRIGGER MY EMBARRASSMENT SUBROUTINES.>

<I'VE SEEN YOU MOVE QUICK, SONODA-SAN! I'M SURE YOU CAN-->
<NO!! ARE YOU CRAZY??>
<IF YOU FIRST PUT MINE ON OVER YOURS, THEN NO ONE WOULD SEE-->
<HOW CAN YOU POSSIBLY THINK MY SKIRT WOULD FIT YOU??>
<IT'S TIGHT, EVEN ON ME.>
<I'M SORRY, PING-SAN.>
<THANK YOU...>
<FOR TRYING TO HELP ME.>
FLIP
<HELLO?>
<N...NANASAWA-SAN?>

MY GOD...
LOOK AT THAT LINE!
I HOPE KIMIKO-SAN ISN'T IN THERE...
BUT WHAT IF SHE IS?
<EXCUSE ME, PARDON ME.>
<I JUST NEED TO-->
<HEY!>
<SIR, PLEASE GO TO THE END OF THE LINE!>
<THERE ARE ALREADY MANY CUSTOMERS WAITING TO BE SERVED. YOU WILL HAVE TO WAIT YOUR TURN!>
<BUT I DON'T, I JUST-->
<IDIOT! ARE YOU TRYING TO CAUSE A RIOT??>
<GO TO THE BACK DOOR, I'LL LET YOU IN.>
<EVERYONE, THANK YOU FOR YOUR PATIENCE, WE WILL BE SERVING YOU SOON!>

<NO, NO, PLEASE DON'T BE UPSET. IT'S NOT YOUR FAULT.>
<THANK YOU... THANK YOU FOR TELLING ME.>
<BYE.>
<NANA-SAWA?>
<TSURA-MURA AND AOI BOTH CALLED IN.>
<WHERE HAVE YOU BEEN???>
<SHE'S BEEN TRYING TO CALL YOU!>
EXIT
<THE RESTAURANT IS FULL OF OTAKU ASKING FOR HER! IT'S CREEPY!>
<I TRIED TO GET HER TO LEAVE, BUT SHE'S BEING STUBBORN!>
<SHE SAYS SHE HAS TO FACE THEM AND IS WORKING HERSELF UP TO IT.>
<YOU'VE GOT TO TALK TO HER! GET HER OUT OF HERE!>
<IT'S JUST YOU AND SAWATARI TONIGHT.>
<I'D SEND YOU HOME, BUT-->
<NO, IT'S OK.>
<I'LL GO.>
<MANAGER-SAN!>
<SAWA-TARI? WHAT ARE YOU DOING? WHO IS THIS?>
<WHERE'S NANASAWA?>
<SHE JUST WENT IN.>
<EHHHH??? YOU SENT HER OUT THERE BY HERSELF??>
<HOW COULD YOU??>
<I-->
<NANA-SAWA~!!>
<SIR, I UNDERSTAND YOU NEED HELP TONIGHT.>

<STOP PUSHING!>
<IS THAT HER?>
-MURMUR-
OOF!>
-RUSTLE-
-MURMUR-
-CLICK-
<REALLY? SHE'S COMING OUT
<NANASAWA! WAIT!>
<YOUR-->
SMASH!!
<EXCUSE ME!!>
<PLEASE DON'T LEAN ON THE DISPLAY CASES!!>
<SORRY!!>

A PREGNANCY SCARE?
IT WAS A LITTLE OVER THREE YEARS AGO, RIGHT AFTER MY FIRST CD CAME OUT.
IT WOULD HAVE BEEN A DISASTER FOR MY CAREER.
BUT WHEN THE TESTS CAME BACK NEGATIVE, I WAS SURPRISED TO FIND I WAS...
DISAPPOINTED.
SO THE ABJECT TERROR OF SPAWNING GAVE YOU AN ACUTE GRRLY MENTAL IMBALANCE.
NO, IT DID NOT.
I'D JUST...
NEVER THOUGHT ABOUT IT BEFORE.
DID YOU BREAK HIM IN HALF FOR KNOXORING JOO UP?
NO, I DIDN'T BREAK HIM IN HALF!!
CRINK
BUT IT DID BREAK THINGS...
IN A WAY.
I GOT EXCITED ABOUT THE IDEA OF HAVING A FAMILY.
HIS BROTHER HAS TWO CHILDREN, MY FUTURE NIECE AND NEPHEW. I WANTED TO GET TO KNOW THEM, TO PLAN AHEAD TO OUR OWN FAMILY.
THEN HITOSHI TOLD ME IT WASN'T POSSIBLE.
HE SAID THAT HIS BROTHER AND HIS WIFE WERE CONCERNED ABOUT THE HARM SOMEONE LIKE ME COULD DO TO THEIR CHILDREN.
HE SAID THAT WHAT I HAD BECOME WAS UNHEALTHY FOR YOUNG, FRAGILE, GROWING MINDS.
SO HE GAVE YOU AN "M FOR M4TUR3" RATING. THAT'S COOL.
WHY AM I TALKING TO YOU ABOUT THIS??

HE LIED TO ME, HE LIED ABOUT ME.
WHY WOULD HE DO THAT? DID HE THINK I WAS A BAD PERSON?
WAS HE ASHAMED OF ME?
WHEN HE LEFT ME, HE SAID IT WAS BECAUSE HE WAS HOLDING ME BACK.
HE SAID I COULD FIND SOMEONE BETTER, SOME-ONE WHO DESERVED ME.
BUT AT THE TIME, I COULDN'T HELP BUT THINK...
HE REALLY WAS TALKING... ABOUT HIMSELF.
AND NOW...
I KNOW HE WAS.
KTHUNK
BLOOD-SUCKING L33CH.
-CRINK-
WHAT?!? H...HOW COULD YOU SAY THAT ABOUT ME?? I--
NOT YOU.
YOU DROPPED YOUR BEER.
L33CHES JOIN PARTIES ONLY TO SERVE THEIR OWN NEEDS.
THEY CAN SUCK THE LIFE OUT OF ANY QUEST.
-FSHP!-
THEIR PASSING SHOULD NOT BE MOURNED.
HERE.

-FSHWIP-
THERE ARE MANY KINDS OF WOUNDS.
BUT TO TAKE DAMAGE FROM SOMEONE YOU TRUST...
BETRAYAL IS THE DEEPEST WOUND OF ALL.
I HAVE SEEN WHAT IT CAN DO TO A WARRIOR'S SOUL.

-CLICK-
<CAN I GET YOUR AUTOGRAPH NANASAWA-SAN?>
<COULD YOU SIGN THIS LIMITED EDITION KOTONE PVC FIGURE?>
<WOW, SHE'S REALLY CUTE IN REAL LIFE, ISN'T SHE?>
<YEAH...>
<UHM, I... I HAVE TO TAKE CARE OF OTHER CUSTOMERS FIRST. MAYBE LATER, OK?>
<ANYONE ELSE NEED-->
<IT WOULD ONLY TAKE A MOMENT! I HAVE A PEN!>
CRASH!
<REHH??>
<I'M SORRY!>
<NO, THIS ISN'T NANASAWA'S SECTION! WHAT CAN I GET YOU?>
<I'LL BE RIGHT THERE!>
<THIS WAS REALLY HARD TO FIND, BUT YOU HAD A SMALL PART IN IT...>
CRASH!
SPLASH!
<AHH!! MY ICED TEA! IT JUST FELL OFF THE TABLE!>
<OH NO!! MY LAP! IT'S SOAKED! HELP!>
<COULD I GET A REFILL ON MY COFFEE, NANASAWA-SAN?>
<JUST A MOMENT, I HAVE TO CLEAN UP THE BROKEN-->
<I, I...>
<COULD I GET ANOTHER WATER?>
<CAN I TAKE A PICTURE? CAN YOU STRIKE A CUTE POSE?>
<I'LL GET IT, NANASAWA-SAN.>
FWIP
THONK
UWAH!
THUNK!
<UHM... HEY.>
<HELLO.>

<P... PIRO-SAN...>
<YOU, UH, REALLY SHOULD BE MORE CAREFUL, NANASAWA-SAN.>
<I TRIED TO CALL YOU.>
<YOU DID? I COULDN'T FIND MY CELL PHONE ANYWHERE.>
<BUS BOY-SAN~~!>
<IT'S SO NICE OF YOU TO COME IN, EVEN THOUGH YOU WEREN'T SCHEDULED TO WORK TODAY.>
<DON'T YOU THINK, NANASAWA-SAN?>
<CLEANUP ON TABLES 14, 23 19 AND 6.>
HAI!
<LET'S RELOAD YOU WITH SOME FRESH POTS, SHALL WE?>
H... HAI.

<NANASAWA, ARE YOU TRYING TO GET HIM KILLED?? USE YOUR HEAD!>
<WHEN DID HE GET HERE?? WHAT'S HE DOING BUSSING TABLES??>
<I HAVE NO IDEA! HE MUST HAVE ASKED MANAGER-SAN IF HE COULD HELP.>
<HE JUST SHOWED UP AT THE FRONT DOOR, ALMOST GAVE ME A HEART ATTACK.>
<I BROUGHT HIM AROUND BACK SO HE COULD SNEAK YOU OUT OF HERE, BUT NOO~~!>
<IT SEEMS YOU'RE BOTH IDIOTS.>
<UHM... NANASAWA-SAN SAID SHE WAS GOING TO CLEAN THAT UP.>
<I'M JUST TAKING CARE OF IT FOR HER.>
<HE HAS SOME NERVE, BEING ON FAMILIAR TERMS WITH NANASAWA-SAN!>
<DO YOU THINK I SHOULD TELL HER ABOUT MY PROBLEMS?>
<I THINK THE UNIFORMS HERE SUIT HER WELL!>
<I'LL ACCIDENTALLY KNOCK THIS OVER WHEN SHE WALKS PAST, THEN SHE'LL HAVE TO BEND DOWN AND...>
<THE WAY SHE WEARS HER SOCKS IS SO CUTE!!>
<A FOREIGNER TOO!!>
<BUT IF NANASAWA-SAN LOVES ALL OF US, IT'S OK, RIGHT?>
<HERE, LOOK AT THIS!!>
<NANASAWA, WHEN THESE FANBOYS START DOING THE KINDS OF THINGS THEY ALWAYS DO, AND YOUR BOYFRIEND GETS ALL PROTECTIVE, ALL HELL IS GONNA-->
<RELAX, MEGUMI, IT'LL BE OK.>
<HE'S A FANBOY TOO.>
<HE KNOWS WHAT HE'S DOING.>
<FOLLOW THE LINE OF HER INNER THIGH... SUCH A DELICATE CURVE...>
<LET ME SEE.>
<THE FOCUS ISN'T REALLY ON LEGS RIGHT NOW, BUT HERS ARE AWESOME.>
<UWAHH... I REALLY HOPE SHE DOES A PHOTOBOOK.>
<ME TOO. I WANT TO SEE HER IN A WHITE SWIMSUIT.>
<UWAH!! I DON'T THINK I COULD HANDLE THAT!>

WAS THAT WHAT I THINK IT WAS?
<I'M STILL AMAZED BY IT ALL.>
<RESEARCH TRIPS HERE HAVE ALWAYS BEEN WORTH IT JUST FOR SAWATARI'S IMPRESSIVE MEASUREMENTS.>
<BUT TO LEARN THAT ONE OF OUR OWN GIRLS IS NOW A FAMOUS SEIYUU...>
<IT'S LIKE WE'VE WATCHED HER GROW.>
<YOU MEAN SHRINK, RIGHT? SHE USED TO WEAR SHAPED INSERTS.>
<AH, BUT NOW WE CAN WONDER AT THEIR SUBTLE BEAUTY...>
<EXCUSE ME.>
<DO YOU HAVE ANY... DIRTY DISHES I CAN TAKE CARE OF?>
<NO. WE HAVE NOT EATEN YET.>
<OH, OK. SORRY! THANK YOU!>
<I DO NOT LIKE HIM. THERE IS SOMETHING CREEPY ABOUT HIM.>
<HE KICKED THE BAG WITH THE CAMERA BACK UNDER THE TABLE.>
<IT LANDED BACK HERE. LET ME SLIDE IT BACK TO YOU.>

I HAD LOST MY ENTIRE LEGION. THE DARK HORDE HAD OVERWHELMED AND DESTROYED THEM.
YET AS I LOOKED BACK, A LONE FIGURE EMERGED FROM THE MIST THAT HAD ONCE BEEN A KINGDOM.
I HAD COME TO DESTROY HER, TO RAVAGE HER LANDS AND PUT HER PEOPLE TO THE SWORD.
BUT NOW HER REALM WAS GONE, THE VERY LAND UPON WHICH IT STOOD COLLAPSING INTO THE ENDLESS MIST.
HOW SHE SURVIVED I DID NOT KNOW.
IS SHE THE ONE WHO BETRAYED YOU?
NO.
I WAS NOT THE ONE WHO WAS BETRAYED.
I COULD HAVE ENDED OUR LONG BATTLE RIGHT THERE.
A CRUSHING BLOW TO HER TINY FRAME.
SHE STOOD THERE, QUIET, DEFIANT, ASKING NO QUARTER.
SHE WAS DAMAGED. SHE WAS WEAK.
DAMAGED... BUT NOT BROKEN.

WAIT, LET ME GET THIS STRAIGHT.
YOU FIGHT THIS BIG BATTLE TO DESTROY THIS WOMAN, THEN LOSE YOUR OWN ASS WHEN THIS "DARK HORDE" MOVES IN AND TAKES BOTH OF YOU OUT.
SO WHY TEAM UP WITH HER? IF SHE DIDN'T HAVE ANYTHING YOU WANTED ANYMORE, WHY BURDEN YOURSELF?
OR DO YOU JUST HAVE A THING FOR DAMAGED GOODS?
DAMAGED GOODS?
DAMAGE CAN BE HEALED.
SHE SOON BECAME A FORMIDABLE ALLY. OF PARTICULAR USE WAS HER ABILITY TO SEE AND SENSE 3VIL WHERE I COULD NOT.
FWSHHHH
YEARS OF RULE HAD WEAKENED HER SKILLZ, BUT IT WAS NOT LONG BEFORE SHE REGAINED THEM.
SHE WAS ALSO A POWERFUL HEALER.
WHAT SHE LACKED IN PHYSICAL PROWESS SHE MADE UP FOR IN MAGICAL ABILITY.
HER SKILLZ AT HEALING WERE VERY USEFUL BECAUSE HER SPELLS HAD A TENDENCY TO ALMOST KILL ME.
FWKOOM
I CAN'T IMAGINE WHY.

WE WERE JOINED BY MANY WHO SOUGHT TO BATTLE THE GROWING EVIL.
BUT THEY WERE OFTEN WEAK AND HAD FEW SKILLZ.
I BET YOU GUYS COULD BATTLE THOSE!
PUNT!
MOST DID NOT SURVIVE THE HARSH JOURNEY.
UNTIL HE JOINED OUR PARTY.
NICE PUNT.
HE WAS NO L33CH. HE HAD RAW ABILITY AND WAS A QUICK LEARNER. HE HAD THE MAKINGS OF A STRONG WARRIOR AND A POWERFUL MAGICIAN. HE FOUGHT BACK TO BACK WITH US AND HELPED US WIN MANY VICTORIES.
HE WAS OPEN AND SHARED ALL THAT HE HAD. HE LEARNED FROM US. WE LEARNED FROM HIM.
HE COULD BACK ME UP IN WAYS SHE COULD NOT. HE COULD HELP HER IN WAYS I COULD NOT.
THERE WAS NO WAY WE COULD HAVE FORESEEN...
THAT THIS WOULD ALL LEAD TO AN 3VIL BETRAYAL.

I DO NOT KNOW EXACTLY WHAT HAPPENED...
OR WHAT MANNER OF SPELLS WERE USED.
BUT THEY WERE POWERFUL SPELLS.
SPELLS THAT OVERPOWERED HER DEFENSES.
SPELLS OF THE DEEPEST, MOST 3VIL MAGIC.
MAGIC THAT BROKE HER WARRIOR SOUL...
AND LAID A PATH TO MY DOOM.

FWIP FWIP FWIP
YOU!!
YOU ARE T3H 3VIL!!
HEAR ME!!
I PH34R NOT YOUR FACELESS MINIONS!!
I AM YOUR DOOM!! FACE ME AND FEEL MY SWORD!!
YOU ARE NOT WORTHY OF EFFORT.
BEGONE.
CRACKLE
I SHALL SEND YOU SPUTTERING INTO THE VOID!!
CLANG!
CRING!! CLANG!! KRANG!!

SUCH A WORTHLESS BRUTE.
YOUR LITTLE GAME IS OVER.
GRRRRRAH!
FWSHANG!
HNNN...
SHFFFF!

HNN...
IDIOT!!!
THIS WASN'T YOUR BATTLE!! WHY DIDN'T YOU RUN??
I TOLD YOU TO RUN!!
I KILLED IT... I DESTROYED... T3H 3VIL...
VNNNVNN
IDIOT.
LOOK WHAT HE DID TO YOU.
YOU STUPID IDIOT...
VNNNVNN
I HAVE DONE WHAT I CAN. YOU MUST REST NOW.
SLEEP. TIME WILL HEAL.

ARE YOU... TRYING TO SAVE ME?
VNNNVNN
YOU... ARE ALMOST SPENT... YOU WILL HURT... YOURSELF IF--
SHUT UP.
VNNNVNN
HNNNN.
VNNN....VN.
shff!
CHINK.
FSHINK!

NNNGG....
SO... HE BETRAYED HER.
SHE HEALED HIM AND THEN HE--
NO.
SHE WAS BETRAYED BY HER "FEELINGS."
HER FEELINGS.
SHE KNEW IT WAS T3H 3VIL BEFORE I DID. ALONE SHE SET OUT TO DESTROY IT. ALONE SHE BATTLED IT UNTIL SHE HERSELF WAS ALMOST DESTROYED.
YET IN THE END SHE COULD NOT LET IT DIE. SHE SAVED IT.
WHY? BECAUSE SHE LET THESE "FEELINGS" AND "EMOTIONS" BE MANIPULATED BY T3H 3VIL, FORCING HER TO ABANDON ALL REASON!
SHE SAVED WHAT SHOULD HAVE BEEN SENT SCREAMING INTO THE ABYSS!!
KRACK!
"EMOTIONS." "FEELINGS."
THEY ONLY LEAD TO DAMAGE, DEATH AND DESTRUCTION.
WOUNDS FROM WITHIN...

WELL EXCUSE ME FOR HAVING FEELINGS!
IT MUST BE NICE TO NEVER HAVE TO BOTHER WITH THEM!
BESIDES, WHAT A LOAD OF BULL!
YOU JUST ACTED OUT THAT ENTIRE STORY WITH THE FLAMBOYANT IDIOCY OF A FIRST YEAR DRAMA STUDENT.
ARE YOU SAYING YOU DON'T HAVE ANY FEELINGS ABOUT WHAT HAPPENED TO YOU?
THE HELL YOU DON'T!!
FEH. YOU'RE PROBABLY JUST PISSED OFF BECAUSE SHE FELL IN LOVE WITH HIM INSTEAD OF YOU.
OH, I'M SORRY, WHAT A HORRIBLE THOUGHT!!
IMAGINE THE HORROR OF HAVING FEELINGS FOR SOMEONE!
BUT THAT NEVER HAPPENS TO YOU, DOES IT, MISTER "WARRIOR?" IT MUST FEEL GOOD TO NEVER CARE ABOUT ANYTHING!!
OF COURSE I CARED!! DO YOU THINK I ENJOYED GETTING SCREWED OVER LIKE THAT? DOES ANYONE ENJOY AN HONORLESS DEATH??
AT LEAST I DON'T WALLOW IN IT!!
SNIFF

-SNIFF-
DAMNIT...
STOP MAKING ME CRY.
JERK.
NOT A LOT OF FUN, AM I?
KINDA LIKE ONE OF THOSE REALLY AWFUL GAMES.
YOU KNOW THE KIND.
IT LOOKS LIKE IT SHOULD BE GOOD, BUT THEN WHEN YOU PLAY IT...
YOU FIND OUT HOW AWFUL IT REALLY IS.
A GAME NOT WORTH PLAYING.
I DON'T PLAY GAMES THAT AREN'T WORTH PLAYING.
UWAHH--GG!! -SNIFF-
DAMNIT!!
STOP IT!!
STOP WHAT???
IDIOT. -SNIFF-

<SEE? HE DISABLED ANOTHER ONE.>
<HE KNOWS EXACTLY WHAT TO LOOK FOR.>
<IS HE HER SECURITY DETAIL?>
<SORRY! SORRY!>
<HEY!>
<NO, HE'S NOT SECURITY.>
<REAL SECURITY WOULD NEVER ALLOW THIS KIND OF ACCESS.>
<NANASAWA-SAN IS WORKING AS A REAL WAITRESS. SHE DOES NOT WANT TO ACT FOR US. SHE WANTS TO BE REAL FOR US.>
<REAL GIRLS DO NOT HAVE SECURITY.>
<SO WHO IS HE?>
<A FAN.>
<A FAN WHO IS TRYING TO "PROTECT" HER AND PRETEND THAT HE IS BETTER THAN THE REST OF US.>
<A FAN WHO WILL TURN HER AGAINST US IN ORDER TO FULFILL HIS OWN SELFISH DESIRES.>
<WE MUST NOT LET THIS HAPPEN.>
<NANA-SAWA-SAN BELONGS TO ALL OF US.>
<HI! I'M SORRY!! I HAVEN'T FORGOTTEN! I'LL BE BACK WITH YOUR EXTRA SAUCE IN A MOMENT!>
<THAT'S OK.>
<TAKE YOUR TIME.>
<THANK YOU.>
<WE ARE IN NO HURRY.>
<MUTO? KURO.>
<YOU ARE IN THE BOOTH NEXT TO US.>
<I AM CALLING IN A FAVOR.>

DAMNIT, WHY DID LARGO HAVE TO BREAK MY GLASSES?
I TOOK CARE OF ALL THE ONES I COULD SEE.
...BUT WHAT ABOUT THE ONES THEY JUST STICK INTO THE AISLE WHEN SHE--
GEH!
<MORE COFFEE?>
<YES, THANK YOU!>
<OK, NEXT TABLE WANTED EXTRA SAUCE...>
<W... WAIT!>
<HERE YOU GO!>
<THANK YOU.>
<MORE COFFEE?>
THUMP!
CRASH!!

<PI-->
<OH MY GOD!!>
CLATTER!
SWISH
<YOU'RE BLEEDING!!>
FWISH
<I'M SORRY! PLEASE, DON'T-->
STOPU!!
<NANASAWA-SAN, DO NOT WASTE THE PURITY OF YOUR ATTENTION ON THIS PERSON!>
<WE SAW IT. AS HE FELL, HE REACHED OUT TO GRAB YOU.>
<HE FAKED THAT FALL SO HE COULD TOUCH YOU IN INAP-PROPRIATE WAYS!>
<WHAT??>
<HE IS TRYING TO TAKE ADVANTAGE OF YOUR PURE HEART FOR HIS OWN SELFISH, PERVERTED DESIRES!>
<I'M TRYING TO TAKE ADVANTAGE OF HER?? ME???>
<YOU'VE GOT SOME NERVE ACCUSING ME OF THAT!! YOU PEOPLE ARE THE ONES WHO ARE TRYING TO... TO...>
<TO...>
THUMP
fzzip

<IF I REALLY WAS A GIRL WITH A PURE HEART, MAYBE I WOULDN'T BE UPSET ABOUT ALL THESE CAMERAS PEOPLE HAVE BEEN TRYING TO POINT UP MY SKIRT.>
<MAYBE I'D BE TOO BUSY SERVING YOU TO NOTICE.>
<MAYBE I'D BE TOO INNOCENT TO UNDERSTAND WHY YOU WOULD WANT PICTURES LIKE THIS.>
<OR MAYBE, IF MY HEART WERE REALLY PURE, I'D UNDERSTAND THAT IT'S JUST PART OF HOW YOU MAKE ME PART OF YOUR FANTASIES.>
<I'D FEEL HONORED BY THE ATTENTION.>
<LOVED, EVEN.>
<I WOULDN'T KNOW.>
<MY HEART ISN'T VERY PURE.>
<YOU'VE ALREADY GOT ONE PICTURE OF MY UNDERWEAR FOR YOUR FANTASIES.>
<IS IT NOT ENOUGH? DO YOU REALLY NEED MORE??>
<IS IT REALLY THAT IMPORTANT TO YOU??>

<MOVE! I CAN'T SEE!>
<OHMYGOD, IS SHE REALLY GONNA DO IT?>
SHFF!
SHFF!
SHFF!
SHFF!
KLANG!
SHFF!
FAF!
<SAWATARI-SAN, I'M GOING ON BREAK.>

<D... DID YOU SEE THAT? SHE ACTUALLY LIFTED IT SEVERAL CENTIMETERS.>
<DON'T YOU THINK SHE LOOKED... UPSET?>
<I WAS TOO AFRAID TO TAKE A PICTURE, DID YOU GET IT?>
<HOW QUICK CAN WE GET A FULL WRITE UP OF THIS ONLINE?>
<EXCUSE ME.>
SKISHH.
<NO ONE IS LEAVING HERE WITH ANY PICTURES. PLEASE PUT DV TAPES AND MEMORY CARDS IN THE BIN.>
<PIRO-SAN, NO-->
<WHAT?>
<YOU WANT ACCESS TO WHAT WE COLLECTED? GO THROUGH NORMAL CHANNELS.>
SMASH!
<SONY DSC-T30/B IN YOUR FRONT POCKET.>
<MEMORY STICK OR CAMERA, YOUR CHOICE.>

<I STILL CAN'T BELIEVE YOU MANAGED TO SCARE SO MANY OF THEM INTO GIVING YOU THEIR MEMORY CARDS.>
<I GUESS DEEP DOWN THEY REALLY ARE ALL JUST A BUNCH OF PATHETIC COWARDS.>
<GOOD THING, TOO. CAN YOU IMAGINE WHAT THE WORLD WOULD BE LIKE IF THEY WEREN'T?>
<SCARY.>
<ANYWAY, GOOD NIGHT! MAKE SURE KIMIKO GETS HOME SAFE, PIRO-SAN!>
<OK, YEAH. I WILL. G' NIGHT.>
<UHM...>
<K... KIMIKO-SAN?>

<WOW.>
<I... I CAN'T BELIEVE-->
<YES YOU CAN.>
<IT WAS JUST AS BAD AS YOU SAID IT WOULD BE. I WAS STUPID AND NAIVE TO EXPECT ANYTHING DIFFERENT.>
<GO AHEAD AND SAY IT.>
<IT WAS STUPID TO THINK THAT THEY'D RESPECT MY FEELINGS.>
<NO! I WASN'T GONNA-->
<IT WAS STUPID TO THINK THEY WOULDN'T PUSH ASIDE MY FEELINGS THE SAME WAY THEY'D LIFT UP MY SKIRT.>
<NOTHING MORE THAN CUTE FRILLS THAT ARE EXCITING TO PUSH ASIDE.>
<OF COURSE, I CAN ALWAYS COUNT ON YOU TO BEAT UP ANYONE WHO TRIES, RIGHT?>

<WH... WHAT?>
<BUT... I DIDN'T...>
<KIMIKO-SAN, I'M SORRY!>
<I DIDN'T MEAN TO BREAK THAT GUY'S CAMERA, IT'S JUST... YOU WERE SO UPSET AND I-->
<AND WHAT, THAT MAKES IT OK?>
<IF I'M STUPID ENOUGH TO BELIEVE THESE PEOPLE MIGHT APPRECIATE MY INNER FEELINGS AND NOT JUST USE THEM AS FLUFF IN THEIR SEXUAL FANTASIES, THAT'S MY PROBLEM!!>
<I'M SORRY! I DIDN'T... I DIDN'T MEAN TO-->
<OF COURSE, IT'S ALL MY FAULT FOR BEING SO DESPERATE TO TALK TO YOU.>
<SOUNDING SO STUPID AND WEAK AND PATHETIC AND SCARED...>
<I BET YOU COULDN'T GET DOWN HERE FAST ENOUGH.>
FSHH
<OF COURSE! I WAS WORRIED ABOUT YOU!!>
<COULDN'T WAIT TO COME DOWN HERE AND "SAVE" ME!>
<SAVE ME FROM MYSELF AND MY PATHETIC DELUSIONS, SCORE SOME POINTS BY BEATING UP A BUNCH OF WEAK, PATHETIC FANBOYS...>
<YOU PROBABLY EVEN THOUGHT IT'D HELP YOU GET LAID TONIGHT!>

<I DIDN'T DESERVE THAT.>
SHHHHTH
THUNK

CHAPTER 7 - END

REAL LIFE ADVENTURES OF PIRO & SERAPHIM SPECIAL! - TREE FREE, CLOTHING FREE!

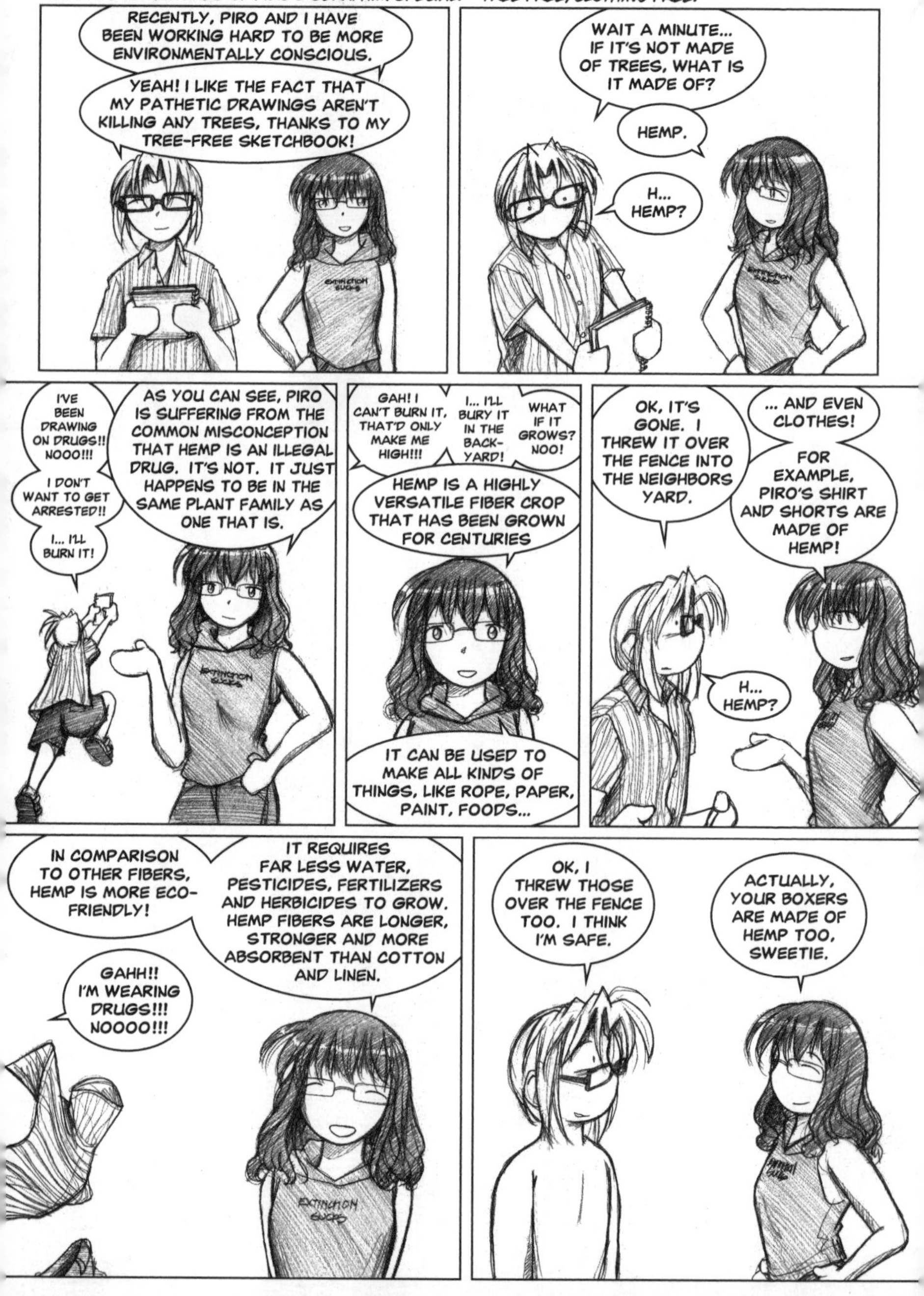

RECENTLY, PIRO AND I HAVE BEEN WORKING HARD TO BE MORE ENVIRONMENTALLY CONSCIOUS.
YEAH! I LIKE THE FACT THAT MY PATHETIC DRAWINGS AREN'T KILLING ANY TREES, THANKS TO MY TREE-FREE SKETCHBOOK!
WAIT A MINUTE... IF IT'S NOT MADE OF TREES, WHAT IS IT MADE OF?
HEMP.
H... HEMP?
I'VE BEEN DRAWING ON DRUGS!! NOOO!!!
I DON'T WANT TO GET ARRESTED!!
I... I'LL BURN IT!
AS YOU CAN SEE, PIRO IS SUFFERING FROM THE COMMON MISCONCEPTION THAT HEMP IS AN ILLEGAL DRUG. IT'S NOT. IT JUST HAPPENS TO BE IN THE SAME PLANT FAMILY AS ONE THAT IS.
GAH! I CAN'T BURN IT, THAT'D ONLY MAKE ME HIGH!!!
I... I'LL BURY IT IN THE BACK-YARD!
WHAT IF IT GROWS? NOO!
HEMP IS A HIGHLY VERSATILE FIBER CROP THAT HAS BEEN GROWN FOR CENTURIES
IT CAN BE USED TO MAKE ALL KINDS OF THINGS, LIKE ROPE, PAPER, PAINT, FOODS...
OK, IT'S GONE. I THREW IT OVER THE FENCE INTO THE NEIGHBORS YARD.
... AND EVEN CLOTHES!
FOR EXAMPLE, PIRO'S SHIRT AND SHORTS ARE MADE OF HEMP!
H... HEMP?
IN COMPARISON TO OTHER FIBERS, HEMP IS MORE ECO-FRIENDLY!
IT REQUIRES FAR LESS WATER, PESTICIDES, FERTILIZERS AND HERBICIDES TO GROW. HEMP FIBERS ARE LONGER, STRONGER AND MORE ABSORBENT THAN COTTON AND LINEN.
GAHH!! I'M WEARING DRUGS!!! NOOOO!!!
OK, I THREW THOSE OVER THE FENCE TOO. I THINK I'M SAFE.
ACTUALLY, YOUR BOXERS ARE MADE OF HEMP TOO, SWEETIE.

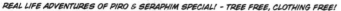

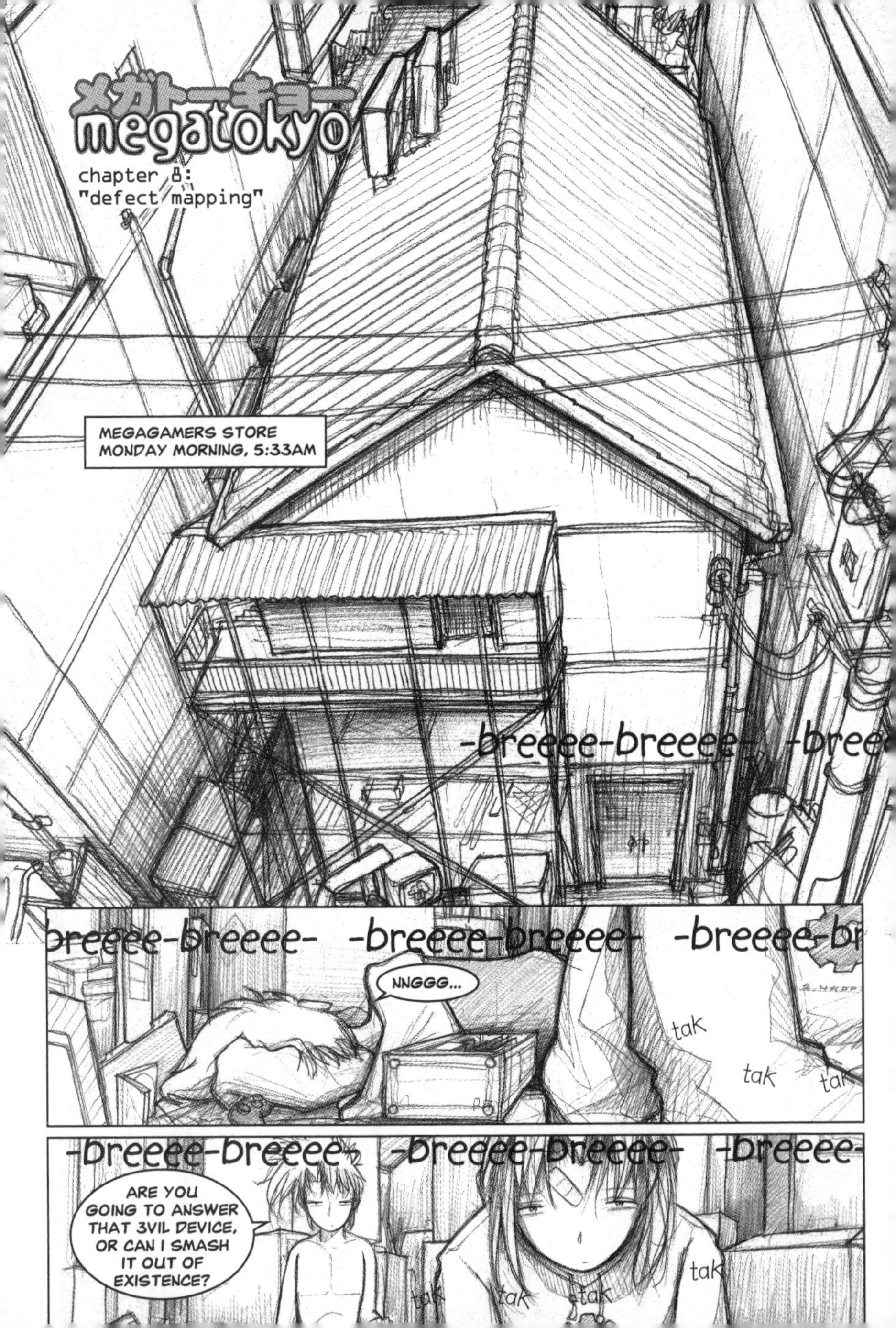

メガトーキョー
megatokyo
chapter 8:
"defect mapping"
MEGAGAMERS STORE
MONDAY MORNING, 5:33AM
-breeee-breeee- -bree
breeee-breeee- -breeee-breeee- -breeee-br
NNGGG...
tak
tak
tak
-breeee-breeee- -breeee-breeee- -breeee-
ARE YOU GOING TO ANSWER THAT 3VIL DEVICE, OR CAN I SMASH IT OUT OF EXISTENCE?
tak
tak
tak
tak

-breeee-breeee-
SIL3NC3! FOUL LINK TO THE UNDER-WORLD!!
-breeee-breeee-
-breeee-
YO.
IT IS AN 3VIL HOUR. WHY ARE YOU AWAKE?
HM.
THAT SOUNDS VERY DANGEROUS.
DO YOU WANT ME TO--
NO?
SMEG
tak tak tak tak
SKRITCH SKRITCH
YEAH, HE'S HERE.
NO, HE'S NOT ALL MO4NY AND W33PY.
JUST GRUMPY AND WUSSY.
HASN'T SAID A WORD SINCE HE GOT IN.
-CLINK-
tak tak taktak tak
RIGHT NOW? HE'S PLAYING SOME GIRLY PORN GAME.
I AM NOT!!!
SMEG

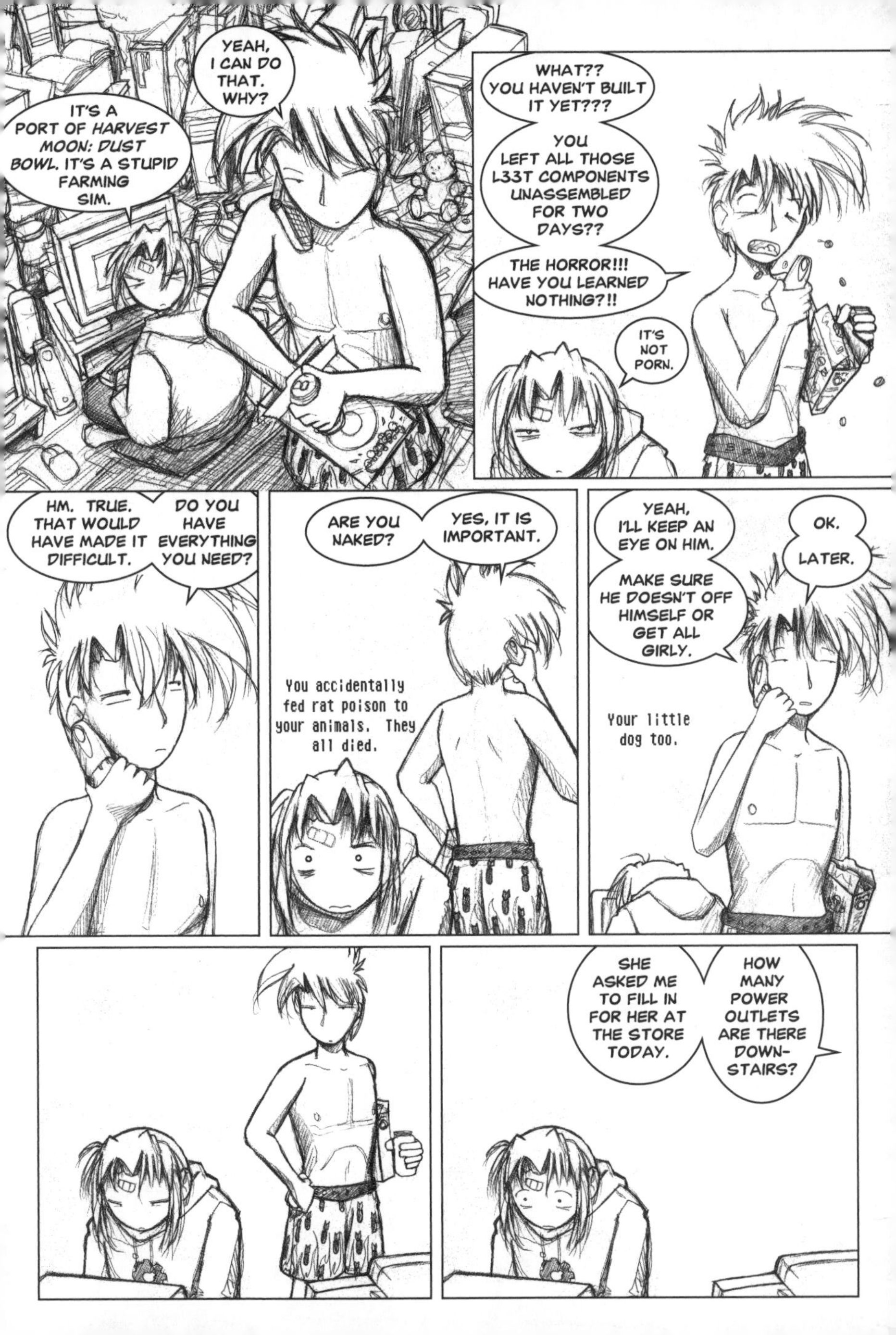
YEAH, I CAN DO THAT. WHY?
IT'S A PORT OF HARVEST MOON: DUST BOWL. IT'S A STUPID FARMING SIM.
WHAT?? YOU HAVEN'T BUILT IT YET???
YOU LEFT ALL THOSE L33T COMPONENTS UNASSEMBLED FOR TWO DAYS??
THE HORROR!!! HAVE YOU LEARNED NOTHING?!!
IT'S NOT PORN.
HM. TRUE. THAT WOULD HAVE MADE IT DIFFICULT.
DO YOU HAVE EVERYTHING YOU NEED?
ARE YOU NAKED?
YES, IT IS IMPORTANT.
You accidentally fed rat poison to your animals. They all died.
YEAH, I'LL KEEP AN EYE ON HIM.
MAKE SURE HE DOESN'T OFF HIMSELF OR GET ALL GIRLY.
OK.
LATER.
Your little dog too.
SHE ASKED ME TO FILL IN FOR HER AT THE STORE TODAY.
HOW MANY POWER OUTLETS ARE THERE DOWN-STAIRS?

<NANA-SAWA.>
<WAKE UP.>
<UHNGWAI!>
FWUFF!
<TH...TH... TH...>
<THAT WAS MEAN!!>
<WAS IT?>
<WOW. YOU LOOK HIDEOUS.>
<NO.>
<LEAVE ME ALONE!!>
<WHATEVER HAPPENED LAST NIGHT, LYING IN BED ALL DAY ISN'T GOING TO HELP YOU GET OVER IT.>
FUMP!
<IT'S 5:45 AM!!!>
<THE DAY IS WASTING AWAY.>
<NOW START TALKING.>

<NO!!>
<GO AWAY!!>
<THE SCHEDULE IN YOUR BAG SAYS YOU NEED TO BE AT THE STUDIO BY 9:30 AM.>
<NO TIME FOR A PITY PARTY.>
<I'M NOT GOING TO THE STUDIO TODAY!>
<I'M **NEVER** GOING BACK TO THE STUDIO!!!>
<LEAVE ME ALONE!!!>
<KIMIKO...>
FUFF!
<WHEN I WAS DISMANTLING MY LIFE A FEW YEARS AGO, THERE WAS A CERTAIN SOMEONE WHO KEPT TRYING TO HELP ME, A PERSON WHO REFUSED TO GIVE UP ON ME.>
<I WAS SO DESPERATE FOR HER TO STOP THAT I BUSTED HER IN THE FACE AND ALMOST KILLED HER.>
<IT DIDN'T STOP HER. SHE NEVER DID GIVE UP ON ME.>
-SNIFF-
<IF I GIVE THIS TO YOU, YOU AREN'T GONNA CHUCK IT AT ME, ARE YOU?>
<NO...>

I MUST SET UP BEFORE THE HORD3 ARRIVES.
<UNYUU... WHY IS EVERYONE UP?>
NO!! I SAID I DON'T NEED YOUR HELP!!
DON'T GO OUT THERE IN YOUR--
PUT SOME PANTS ON!!!
LARGO!!!
<I GUESS I SHOULD GET READY FOR SCHOOL.>
<WHAT-EVER. I DON'T CARE.>
<UWAEH?? WHAT THE? WHY DOESN'T THIS...>
<PIRO-SAN?>
<PIRO-SAN?>
<PIRO-SAN!!! WAHHH!!! HELP!!>
<DAMNIT PING-->
<WHAT?!?>
<MY UNIFORM!>
<IT... IT DOESN'T FIT!!>
<IT FIT THE OTHER DAY!!>
<WHY DOESN'T IT FIT ANYMORE??>
DIDN'T REALIZE THAT THING WAS INFLATABLE.
COO.

NO!! STAY AWAY!!
CRASH!!
THE STATIC-FREE ZONE MUST NOT BE COMPROMISED!!
YOUR STATIC-FREE ZONE WON'T BE ALL I COMPROMISE IF YOU DON'T PUT THESE ON.
DUDE. CHILL.
NO, I WILL NOT CHILL!! I'M TRYING TO KEEP HER FROM KILLING YOU!!
I DETECT NO THREATS.
<UH... PING?>
<LARGO'S... MOSTLY NAKED. WHY AREN'T YOU TRYING TO HURT HIM?>
WOOT! THIS GIGA-BIT CARD IS UNDAMAGED!
<I... I WISH HE'D PUT MORE CLOTHES ON, IT'S REALLY EMBARRASSING, BUT... THAT DOESN'T MEAN I SHOULD HURT HIM.>
<DOES IT?>
EVEN I WANT TO HURT HIM WHEN HE WALKS AROUND LIKE THAT.
OH, YOU'RE JUST JEALOUS OF HOW COMFORTABLE HE IS WITH HIMSELF.

UWAH!!
ACTUALLY, HE'S SURPRISINGLY CUTE IN BOXERS.
WHAT WHATWHAT HOW--
THE DOOR WAS AJAR.
<MIHO-CHAN~!! MY... MY...>
<YES, DEAR, I KNOW. CALM DOWN.>
<I ASKED WALTAH TO LET OUT ONE OF MY UNIFORM TOPS FOR YOU. HE DID WHAT HE COULD. YOU CAN ONLY ALTER THEM SO MUCH.>
<I HOPE IT'S ENOUGH.>
G...GET OUT!! I'M IN NO MOOD FOR YOU TODAY!!
DO YOU TAKE SOME SORT OF PLEASURE IN MAKING GIRLS CRY, PIRO?
<WE ADJUSTED THE WAIST ON THE SKIRT TOO. I ASSUME YOURS IS TOO TIGHT.>
<MIHO-CHAN! H...HOW DID YOU KNOW?>
<YOUR PHYSICAL DIMENSIONS HAVE BEEN CHANGING FOR SEVERAL DAYS NOW.>
<YOUR BUST SIZE IS THE MOST NOTICEABLE CHANGE, BUT YOUR HIPS ARE WIDER AND YOU ARE A BIT TALLER TOO.>
<MOST OF YOUR CLOTHES WON'T FIT RIGHT ANYMORE.>
<MIHO-CHAN...>
<WHAT ARE YOU TALKING ABOUT?>
<YOU DON'T KNOW?>
THAT'S INTERESTING.
YOU LET T3H 3VIL IN.
YOU LEFT THE DOOR OPEN!!

<YOU TRY THOSE ON. I'LL WAIT OUT HERE WITH THE BOYS.>
<OK.>
WH... WHAT DID YOU DO TO PING?!
DON'T LOOK AT ME. YOU'RE THE ONE WHO DIDN'T DO ANYTHING.
WHAT?
PING IS A GAME. SHE'LL NEVER BE MORE THAN A SUBSTITUTE FOR A REAL GIRL.
FOR HER, EVERY GAME SHE PLAYS WILL END IN A BROKEN HEART.
JUST LIKE THE ONE SHE TRIED TO PLAY WITH YOU.
WE ALL REACT TO HEARTACHE IN DIFFERENT WAYS.
SOME DO DRASTIC THINGS, LIKE HURT OURSELVES OR THE PEOPLE AROUND US.
SOME JUST BUY A NEW COMPUTER, CUT OUR HAIR OR EAT A PINT OF ICE CREAM.
PING CAN DO SOMETHING MOST OF US WISH WE COULD DO - SHE CAN ACTUALLY CHANGE HERSELF.
HER HAIR, HER BODY, HER MEMORIES, HER PERSONALITY...
I'M ACTUALLY...
KIND OF JEALOUS.
DUD3. PLAN.
I SET ALL THIS CARDBOARD ON FIRE. YOU MAKE FOR THE TRAP DOOR AND I'LL DIVE THROUGH THE WINDOW.
ONE OF US MIGHT SURVIVE.
MAYBE.

<WOW.>
<TO GO FROM RELATIVE OBSCURITY TO HAVING TO DEAL WITH THAT LEVEL OF FAN BEHAVIOR OVER-NIGHT...>
<KIMIKO, IF ANYONE COULD HAVE HELPED YOU WITH THIS, IT WAS ME.>
<I SHOULD HAVE BEEN THERE FOR YOU. I'M SORRY.>
<YET YOU HANDLED IT WELL.>
<YOU DIDN'T RUN AWAY, YOU MADE YOUR OWN DECISIONS AND YOU STOOD UP FOR YOUR-SELF.>
<THAT'S MORE THAN I EVER DID.>
<AS FOR PIRO...>
<BUSSING TABLES, DISABLING CAMERAS, CONFISCATING, MEMORY CARDS, SMASHING CAM-CORDERS?>
<YOUR BOY MIGHT HAVE A BIT OF A SPINE AFTER ALL.>
<YOU DIDN'T RIP HIS LITTLE SPINE OUT AND STUFF IT DOWN A GARBAGE DISPOSAL, DID YOU?>
<HNGG....>

<WELL?>
<DID HE DESERVE THAT?>
<NO...>
<IF HE'S SMART, HE'LL RUN, AND RUN FAST.>
<I'M SURE HE'S REALIZED THAT THERE'S NO WAY A NICE, QUIET GUY LIKE HIM CAN SURVIVE THE DESTRUCTIVE POWERS OF KIMI-ZILLA.>
<OH DEAR.>
<I FORGOT, YOUR SENSE OF HUMOR IS KINDA BROKEN THIS MORNING.>
<I'M SORRY.>
<UHHNNNGG-WAAHHH!!>
SNIFF!!

SO PING... ISN'T PING ANYMORE?
SHE'S CHANGED... INTO SOMEONE ELSE?
SKSHH
OH, NO. PING IS STILL PING.
SHE JUST...
CHANGED...
A LITTLE.
IF YOU COULD CHANGE SOMETHING ABOUT YOURSELF, WHAT WOULD IT BE?
ASIDE FROM THE OBVIOUS.
THE OBVIOUS??
THERE ARE ALWAYS A LOT OF THINGS WE'D LIKE TO CHANGE ABOUT OURSELVES.
BUT IF YOU COULD CHANGE ONLY ONE THING, DEEP INSIDE, WHAT WOULD IT BE?
SKISH
SKISH
WOULD YOU CHANGE WHAT CAUSED THIS?

WHUH WHUHWHUH THATTHAT WHERE--
<AH, THERE WE GO.>
<DOES IT LOOK OK?>
<IT'S A LITTLE TIGHT.>
<IT LOOKS FINE.>
<CAN'T BELIEVE THAT USED TO BE MY TOP.>
BUH BUH--
<WE HAVE SOME TIME. SHALL WE GET SOME BREAKFAST?>
<CAN I GET WAFFLES?>
<OF COURSE.>
BUH...
<OH! BYE BYE, PIRO-SAN! LARGO-SAN! I'LL SEE YOU AFTER SCHOOL!>
SHFF
KERCHACK..
SLAM
THE CONTAINMENT BARRIER WAS BREACHED.
KERCHACK..
SWISH!

THUMP THUMP! THUMP! MP!
UWAH!
YOU ARE SO CUTE WHEN YOU'RE MAD.
WHERE DID YOU GET THOSE PICTURES?
I TOOK THEM.
I CAN SEND YOU COPIES, IF YOU LIKE.
JOIN US FOR BREAK-FAST?

GUESS I CAN REPURPOSE THIS SYSTEM.

<FEELING ANY BETTER?>
<YOU DO REALIZE...>
<YOU'VE BECOME FAMOUS BY JUST BEING YOURSELF.>
<IT WASN'T BECAUSE OF A PERSONALITY SCRIPTED FOR YOU BY YOUR HANDLERS,>
<OR A PUBLICITY STUNT ARRANGED BY THE STUDIO.>
<IT WAS JUST YOU BEING YOU.>
<I'M KINDA JEALOUS.>
<ERIKA...>
<DON'T EVER LET YOUR HANDLERS CHANGE WHO YOU ARE. JUST KEEP BEING YOURSELF, AND YOU'LL BE FINE.>
<THOUGH YOU MIGHT WANT TO ASK FOR THEIR HELP WITH THIS PIRO THING.>
<YOU BLEW THAT RATHER SPECTACULARLY.>
<UHREEH~>

<YOU KNOW...>
<YOU'D FEEL A LOT BETTER IF YOU JUST CALLED HIM.>
<WEHH?? I... I... I CAN'T! I... HE...>
<KIMIKO...>
<I'M SURE HE'LL UNDER-STAND.>
<CALL ME IF YOU NEED ME.>
<GOOD LUCK.>
<WELL, IT'S NOT GOING TO BUILD ITSELF.>
COMPUDOG

YOU SHOULD EAT SOMETHING, PIRO.
YOU LOOK HUNGRY.
WHY ARE YOU DOING THIS?
DOING WHAT?
DRAGGING ME HERE! TAKING PICTURES OF NANASAWA-SAN CRYING AND SHOVING THEM IN MY FACE!! PLAYING GAMES WITH--
WAS SHE REALLY...
CRYING?
I'VE RARELY SEEN ANYONE THAT UPSET.
CAN YOU TELL ME WHAT HAPPENED LAST NIGHT?
MAYBE I CAN HELP.

HELP??
YOU WANT TO... HELP?
I KNOW WE HAVE A HISTORY, BUT THAT DOESN'T MEAN I WANT YOU TO BE MISERABLE.
I JUST HAPPENED TO BE ON THAT TRAIN LAST NIGHT.
I DIDN'T HEAR EXACTLY WHAT WAS SAID, BUT YOU SAID SOME-THING VERY STERNLY BEFORE LETTING THE DOOR CLOSE BETWEEN YOU.
IT MUST HAVE BEEN HARSH, BECAUSE SHE STOOD THERE GRIPPING THE HAND RAIL, SOBBING, FOR THE ENTIRE TRIP.
I WAS CONCERNED, SO I FOLLOWED HER TO MAKE SURE SHE GOT HOME OK.
IT'S HARD TO WATCH SOMEONE BREAK DOWN IN PUBLIC.
I COULDN'T HELP BUT WONDER WHAT WOULD MAKE YOU HURT AND ABANDON HER LIKE THAT.
WHAT DID SHE DO?
I HAVE TO GO.
<PIRO-SAN!>

大
ON3
YOU'RE FEELING CONFLICTED, AREN'T YOU?
YOU FELT HURT BY WHAT SHE SAID. AFTER ALL YOU WENT THROUGH FOR HER, YOU DIDN'T DESERVE TO BE TREATED LIKE THAT.
YOU SAID SO. YOU STOOD UP FOR YOURSELF.
BUT SHE WASN'T HERSELF LAST NIGHT. SHE WAS UPSET. SHE NEEDED YOU TO BE THERE FOR HER, BUT YOU PUT YOUR OWN FEELINGS FIRST AND ABANDONED HER.
YOU FEEL GUILTY ABOUT IT.
GOTTA ADMIT, THIS IS A TOUGH ONE.

STOP DITHERING AND TALK TO ME.
BIG MODE IS EXPENSIVE.
I... I... I MADE HER CRY--
NO, SHE MADE HERSELF CRY.
SHE'S THE ONE THAT ACCUSED YOU OF BEING ALL MACHO AND BEATING UP FANBOYS SO YOU COULD SCORE WITH HER. IT WAS A NASTY THING TO SAY.
ALL YOU DID WAS STAND UP FOR YOUR-SELF.
OH, THIS IS CUTE.
BESIDES, YOU? MACHO? WAS SHE TRYING TO BE FUNNY?
BUT... WHY DID SHE SAY THAT? WAS I BOTHERING HER TOO MUCH? DID SHE NOT WANT ME THERE? DID I OVERSTEP--
PIRO...
WHY DO YOU INSIST ON EVERYTHING BEING YOUR FAULT?
YOU'RE NOT THE ONLY ONE WHO GETS TO MAKE CHOICES THAT MAKE A RELATIONSHIP WORK OR NOT.
YOU SHOULD WEAR MORE BUTTON DOWN SHIRTS, THEY LOOK GOOD ON YOU.

IT'S OK TO FEEL BAD BECAUSE YOU CARE ABOUT HER, BUT DO **NOT** FEEL BAD ABOUT STANDING UP FOR YOURSELF.
EMOTIONAL ABUSE IS NEVER OK.
SKISH SKISH
AH!
SKISH SKISH
I... I... I LIKE HER.
I DON'T... I DON'T WANT TO GIVE UP ON HER... YET.
I DIDN'T SAY TO GIVE UP ON HER.
JUST DON'T LET HER WALK ALL OVER YOU.
SKISH SKISH SKIS
IT WON'T BE MUCH OF A RELATIONSHIP IF YOU DO.
SO... "BIG MODE" IS EXPENSIVE, HUH?
IT WOULD BE IF THESE STORES CARRIED ANYTHING THAT FIT NORMAL SIZED GIRLS.

<AH, SUCH A NICE DAY.>
<I BET HAYASAKA TOOK THE DAY OFF.>
<WHAT THE...>
PHEER
SHFFF!!
<HAYASAKA!! WHAT'S WITH THE-->
PHEER!
<HELP!!>
whump!
BING!
<I'M SCARED!>
<ALMOST... GOT IT!>
<THIS WAY!!>
<DON'T BE! I GOT YOU COVERED!>
AIEEE!!!
THUMP! THUMP! THUMP!- THUMP THUN
KERSNIP!
<BOXES...?>
<THE CAPSULE TOY MACHINE GOT TSUKASA!!!>
<THERE'S GOT TO BE A WAY TO GET THROUGH!>
<HAYA-SAKA, PLEASE TELL ME YOU'RE HERE.>
<PLEASE.>
PHEER

KYAA!!
<WHAT IS ALL THIS??>
<WHAT ARE YOU DOING?? WHERE'S HAYA-SAKA!?!>
WHAT YOU DO MY STORE!!!!
YO, MANAGER DUDE.
GASP GASP
<I... I MADE IT!>
THIS STORE PRESENTED NO CHALLENGE IN ACQUIRING COVETED ITEMS.
THERE IS NO SATISFACTION IN HAVING THESE ITEMS IF YOU CAN JUST WALK OVER AND TAKE THEM.
<HE DOESN'T SPEAK JAPANESE AT ALL... OH MY GOD...>
<DON'T... PLEASE, JUST STOP WHATEVER YOU ARE DOING...>
STOPU!
PUREEZU, STOPU!!
CHILL A CYCLE, DUDE, PWNZING SOME LUZR.
tak tak tak
<UM, SIR?>
<I MADE IT THRU, CAN I BUY THIS NOW?>
<UWAH! A CUSTOMER!!>
<I'M SORRY SIR! I APOLOGIZE FOR THE DANGEROUS CONDITIONS YOU ENCOUNTERED IN THE STORE TODAY!>
<I WILL PUT AN END TO THIS IMMEDI-ATELY!!>
L33T SHARDZ OF PH33R!!
tak tak tak tak tak tak
<HUH? WHAT ARE YOU TALKING ABOUT?>
<THIS "PH34R!" GAME IS AWESOME! IT'S MY FIFTH TIME THROUGH!>
<I THINK I FIGURED OUT A WAY TO GET PAST THAT "3VIL" CLOTHING RACK ON THE 2ND FLOOR!>
<YAY! NOW I CAN GET THAT SOS-DAN T-SHIRT!!>

KERSNIP!
KERCHACK!
DUDE! THAT **ROXOR3D!**
BUT THIS IS A CONSUMER GRADE LEVEL, NOT NINJ4 GRADE!
AH. JUNPEI WONDER WHY SEEM EASY.
FIXU PURESU?
<A CUSTOMER JUST CALLED SEVERAL OF HIS FRIENDS AND TOLD THEM TO COME.>

L33T MASTER TEACH CLASS, HALF HOUR.
DUDE.
I AM RUNNING A GAME, I CANNOT ABANDON IT.
BEING A GM IS A GREAT RESPONSIBILITY. IT MUST BE TAKEN SERIOUSLY.
JUNPEI TOLD SHIPMENT L33T MASTER REQUEST ARRIVE.
90 AMD ATHLON64 X2 DUAL-CORE PROCESSOR PACK IN DRY ICE AND PART FOR 30 SYSTEM.
GREAT TEACHER LARGO HAS A CLASS TO TEACH!
WAIT! WHERE YOU GO??

FEELING ANY BETTER?
I KIND OF WISH IT REALLY WAS ALL MY FAULT.
OH? WHY IS THAT?
BECAUSE THEN I'D KNOW WHAT TO DO.
I MIGHT NOT BE ABLE TO DO IT, BUT I'D KNOW.
WHICH WOULD MAKE IT EASY TO WIMP OUT AND GIVE UP, RIGHT?
EH?
UWAH!!
CRASH!
<HELP! HELP! HELP!>
fump fump fump fump
PHEER
-GASP!- -GASP!-
<IT... IT... IT GOT ME!>
AH.
SOMETIMES YOU HAVE TO DEAL WITH THINGS EVEN WHEN THEY AREN'T YOUR FAULT.
HAVE FUN!

KERSNIP!
LARGO!!
UWAH!
THUMP THUMP THUMP
<AIEEEE!!!>
<WAHHH!!!>
<NO!! NOT MY HEAD!!! NOOO!!>
I AM GOING...
<OH MY GOD!!! NO!!!>
<HELP!! HELP!!>
<RUN, TAKA, RUN!!>
SWISH!
...TO KILL HIM.
<BOSS-SAN!>
<PIRO-SAN! THANK GOD!>
TAK TAK TAK
<WHERE'S LARGO??>
<SOME NINJA CAME AND TOOK HIM.>
<YOU HAVE TO HELP ME! I CAN'T READ ANY OF THIS!!>
AIEEEE!!!
TAK TAK TAK TAK
THUMP THUMP
<BOSS-SAN, I'M SO SORRY! I'LL CLEAN THIS UP AS SOON AS I-->
<WAIT, I THINK I'M GETTING THE HANG OF-->
TAK TAK TAK TAK TAK TAK TAK TAK TAK TAK
...FIND LARGO AND PK HIM.
<I HAVE NO IDEA WHAT I'M DOING!!>

LARGO SETS UP SOME STUPID GAME, FILLS THE STORE WITH CARDBOARD HAZARDS AND TAKES OFF.
DOES BOSS-SAN GET PISSED? NO! HE LOVES IT! WHAT THE HELL?
RINGRING!
RINGRINGRING!
DIDN'T HAYASAKA-SAN ASK LARGO TO FILL IN FOR HER AT THE STORE TODAY?
I'M SURE SHE'D BE PISSED IF SHE FOUND OUT.
<HELLO, MEGAGAMERS, CAN I HELP YOU?>
FOUND OUT WHAT?
H... H... HAYASAKA-SAN!?
I'M HAVING TROUBLE GETTING THE SETTINGS RIGHT ON THIS THING. WHOEVER WROTE THE MANUAL FOR THIS MOTHERBOARD NEEDS TO BE SHOT.
I ASSUME LARGO UNDER-STANDS THIS GIBBERISH. CAN I TALK TO HIM?
LARGO? HE... HE'S NOT HERE!
HE'S NOT?
SIGH
UHM... I SENT HIM OFF TO DO SOME ERRANDS.
I'VE BUILT A FEW COMPUTERS, CAN I HELP?

<WHAT THE HELL IS WRONG WITH YOUR HEAD?!?>
<IN WHAT UNIVERSE DID YOU THINK IT WOULD BE OK TO WAIT ON A RESTAURANT FULL OF OBSESSIVE, SLAVERING, OTAKU?!?>
<I'M REALLY BEGINNING TO QUESTION YOUR JUDGMENT, NANASAWA-SAN.>
<FIRST THAT STUNT YOU PULLED ON MUMU'S RADIO SHOW AND NOW THIS? WHAT NEXT? START A REVOLUTION AND BURN TOKYO TO THE GROUND?!?>
<NIIDERA-SAN, SHE'S NEW TO THIS. DON'T BE SO HARSH.>
<I'M SORRY, MATSUI-SAN. WE ARE AS MUCH SURPRISED BY HER BEHAVIOR AS YOU ARE. I WILL TALK TO HER.>
<YOU'RE HER AGENT, DON'T JUST TALK TO HER, PUT A DAMN LEASH ON HER!!>
<FIND SOMEONE ELSE.>
<EH? WHAT?>
<IT WAS A MISTAKE TO THINK I WANTED THIS.>
<PLEASE FIND SOMEONE ELSE TO DO THE PART.>

<WHAT?? NOT WHAT YOU WANTED? FIND SOMEONE ELSE? **DON'T GIVE ME THAT CRAP!!**>
<NANA-SAWA, THESE ARE UNNECESSARY THEATRICS.>
<SINCE DAY ONE I'VE BEEN BENDING OVER BACKWARDS TO ACCOMMODATE EVERY ONE OF YOUR MOODY LITTLE WHIMS!>
<STOP YELLING AT ME.>
<IT'S TIME YOU STARTED THINKING ABOUT WHAT I NEED FROM YOU!!>
<I SAID STOP YELLING AT ME.>
<NANA-SAWA-SAN!!>
<YOU CAN PUT A LEASH ON ME IF YOU WANT, MATSUI-SAN...>
<BUT DO YOU REALLY THINK YOU CAN HOLD IT?>

CAPUS
京王クラウン街 高井戸
KEIO 高井戸駅
<THIS...>
<ISN'T...>
<HOW I WANT TO FEEL.>
CLICK
CHACK
<PIRO, IS THAT YOU?>
<EH?>
<TOOK YOU LONG ENOUGH.>
<GET UNDRESSED AND GET IN HERE.>

<NANA-SAWA? WHAT ARE YOU DOING HOME?>
<WHA-- WHA-- WHAT ARE YOU-->
<WHAT?!?>
<TAKE OFF YOUR CLOTHES.>
<ERIKA!, NO!! I DON'T, STOP--!>
<AIIEEE!!!>
<YOU CAN'T GET IT TO WORK?>
<I FOLLOWED ALL THE INSTRUCTIONS AND PORED OVER EVERY MANUAL, I CAN'T FIGURE OUT WHAT'S WRONG.>
<PIRO THINKS I'M MISSING SOME UNDOCUMENTED JUMPER SETTING SOMEWHERE.>
<THAT WASN'T NICE, YOU KNOW.>
<WHAT WASN'T?>
<TEASING ME ABOUT PIRO COMING HERE, AND YOU... AND HE...>
<I WASN'T TEASING. HE'S COMING OVER TO HELP ME FIX THIS THING.>
<SHOULD BE HERE ANY MINUTE.>
CLATTER

<HE'S COMING HERE? RIGHT NOW??>
<HE SAID HE MIGHT BE ABLE TO HELP. I DIDN'T KNOW YOU'D BE HOME EARLY.>
<I HAVE TO GO!!>
<ACTUALLY, WHY ARE YOU HOME EARLY?>
<WHY? ONCE HE HELPS ME GET THIS THING WORKING, YOU GUYS CAN TALK.>
<I'M NOT READY TO TALK TO HIM YET!>
<WHAT DID I TELL YOU ABOUT CLOTHES AND STATIC? DO THAT IN THE HALL-WAY.>
<ANSWER THE DOOR IN YOUR UNDERWEAR. HE WON'T CARE IF YOU'RE READY TO TALK OR NOT.>
<HM?>
<HEY, CAREFUL, YOU'LL MAKE SPARKS.>

I KNOW KIMIKO ISN'T HERE.
I PROBABLY WOULDN'T HAVE COME IF SHE WAS.
BUT I CAN'T SHAKE THIS FEELING THAT WHAT I REALLY WISH...
IS THAT SHE WAS.
OF COURSE I HAVE NO IDEA WHAT I'D SAY, AND IT WOULD BE A TOTAL DIS-ASTER AND I'D SCREW IT UP SO IT'S PROBABLY A GOOD THING SHE--
CRASH!
KTHUMP
thump
thump
thump
thump
click.
<TOOK YOU LONG ENOUGH.>
<NANASAWA IS HIDING IN THE BATHROOM.>
<YOU'LL HAVE TO GET UNDRESSED IN THE HALL-WAY.>

<YOU CAN DROP YOUR CLOTHES RIGHT THERE.>
<UWEH?>
<I HOPE THIS SWIM-SUIT FABRIC DOESN'T GENERATE STATIC.>
<NANA-SAWA MADE ME CHANGE.>
<SEEMS SHE HAS A PROBLEM WITH YOU SEEING ME IN MY UNDER-WEAR.>
<SOME-THING WRONG?>
<IS NANASAWA-SAN...>
<REALLY HERE?>
<WHAT WOULD YOU DO IF SHE WAS?>

<I...>
<I...>
<I'D JUST...>
<TALK TO HER.>
<I WANT TO TALK TO HER.>
<COME ON, LET'S FIX THIS THING.>
<DROP THE CLOTHES AND GET IN HERE.>
<WHY DO I HAVE TO GET UNDRESSED?!>

BECAUSE YOU WILL DESTROY THESE COMPONENTS IF YOU DO NOT!!
EACH OF YOU IS WEARING ENOUGH FABRIC TO GENERATE HORRENDOUS AMOUNTS OF STATIC ELECTRICITY.
THE CLOTHING MUST BE REMOVED.
I WILL ALLOW MINIMAL UNDER-GARMENTS.
GET UNDRESSED AND RETRIEVE YOUR COMPONENTS. WE HAVE MUCH TO DO.
SENSEI! YOU CANNOT ASK US TO GET UNDRESSED IN FRONT OF ALL THESE BOYS!!
<CAN HE REALLY MAKE US DO THIS??>
<EEP!>
<THIS CLASS IS SO AWESOME! HURRY AND GET UNDRESSED!>
<CAN'T WE JUST WEAR ANTI-STATIC WRISTBANDS?>
GENIUS!!
GREAT TEACHER LARGO ROCKSORS!!
<PERVERTS! YOU JUST WANT TO SEE US IN OUR UNDERWEAR!!>
STOP!!
NO! WE MUST PRESERVE THE STATIC OF MAD COMPUTER HACKSOR!!
GIRLS GET NAKED! CLOTHES DESTROY COMPONENT LEETNESS!
I SENSE A LACK OF R3SP3CT.

YOU WOULD DEFILE THE ACT OF ASSEMBLY BY LUSTING AFTER THE FLESH OF A FELLOW HAXOR?
T3H L33TNESS OF THESE CO/\/\PON3NTZ DEMAND YOUR FULL ATTENTION!!
YOUR 3Y3Z WILL SEE NOTHING ELSE!!
RIGHT. WHAT PLANET ARE YOU FROM AGAIN?
HE WON'T UNDER-STAND, CLASS PRESIDENT.
WE AREN'T AS "L33T" AS HE IS.
HE WON'T UNDERSTAND WHY THE BOYS WOULD RATHER LOOK AT ALL OF YOU NAKED THAN OBSESS OVER HIS DUAL CORE PROCESSORS.
ONLY MACHINES HE CAN USE TO LIVE OUT PUFFED UP FANTASIES ABOUT HIMSELF ARE WORTHY OF HIS "L33T" ATTENTION.
I CANNOT RESPECT SOMEONE WHO IS ONLY ATTRACTED TO HIMSELF.
<TOHYA!! SHOW PROPER RESPECT!!>

TOHYA! YOU GO TOO FAR!!
LARGO-SENSEI IS NOT LIKE THAT! HOW DO YOU KNOW HE--
THERE IS A WOMAN I AM ATTRACTED TO.
BUT I DO NOT DISRESPECT HER...
WHEN SHE IS IN PURSUIT OF L33T KNOWLEDGE.
WHAT ABOUT WHEN SHE'S NOT?
I ACCEPT THAT THIS IS A DIFFICULT SKILL TO MASTER.
WHAT ELSE CAN BE DONE TO PROTECT THESE COMPONENTS FROM STATIC DISCHARGE?
TAKE OFF OUR SOCKS?
UHM... ANTI-STATIC WRISTBANDS?
WIRE OURSELVES TO OUR DESKS?
GYM CLOTHES?
IF WE COULD CHANGE IN ANOTHER ROOM...
SWIM-SUITS!!
NO!!

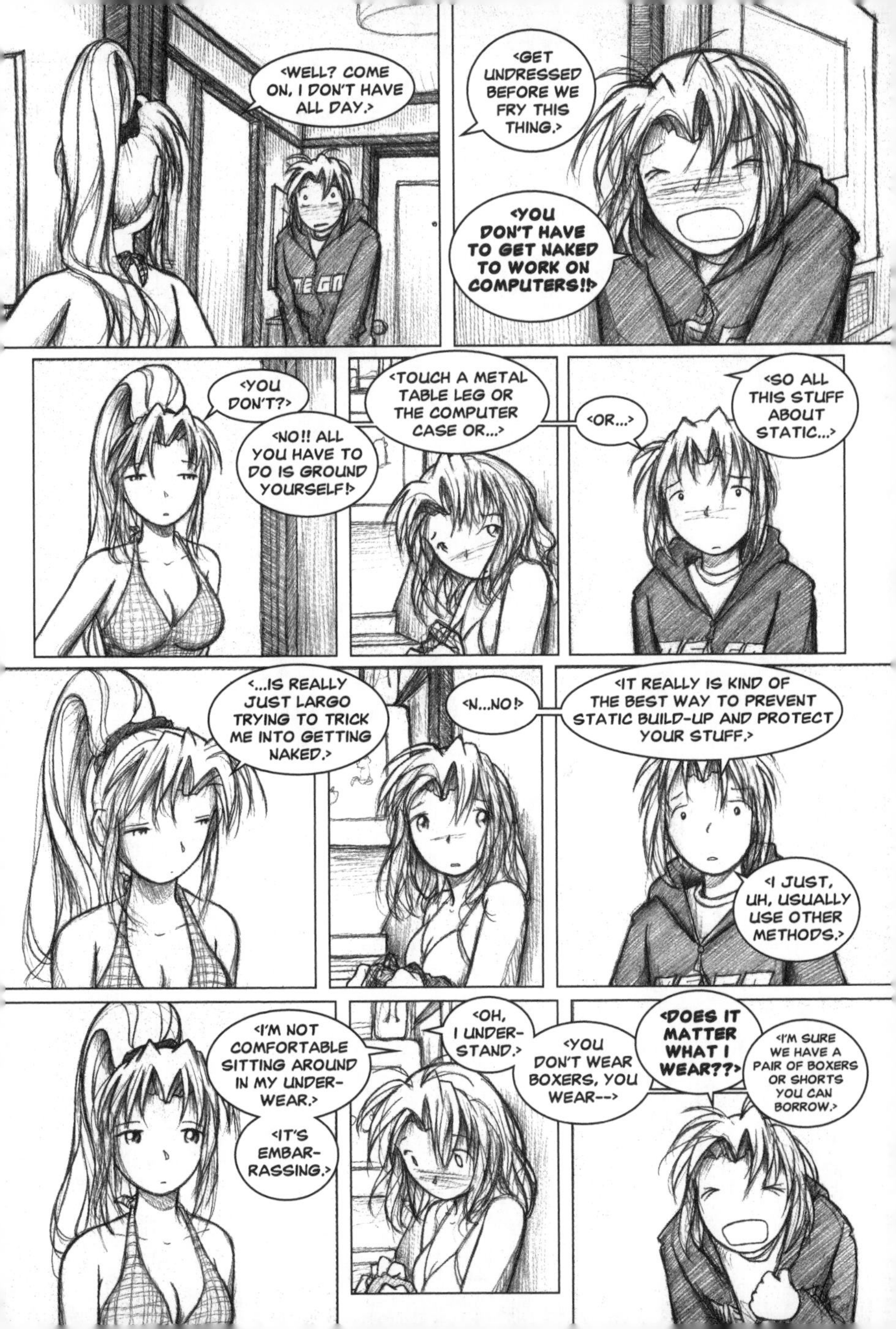
<WELL? COME ON, I DON'T HAVE ALL DAY.>
<GET UNDRESSED BEFORE WE FRY THIS THING.>
<YOU DON'T HAVE TO GET NAKED TO WORK ON COMPUTERS!!>
<YOU DON'T?>
<NO!! ALL YOU HAVE TO DO IS GROUND YOURSELF!>
<TOUCH A METAL TABLE LEG OR THE COMPUTER CASE OR...>
<OR...>
<SO ALL THIS STUFF ABOUT STATIC...>
<...IS REALLY JUST LARGO TRYING TO TRICK ME INTO GETTING NAKED.>
<N...NO!>
<IT REALLY IS KIND OF THE BEST WAY TO PREVENT STATIC BUILD-UP AND PROTECT YOUR STUFF.>
<I JUST, UH, USUALLY USE OTHER METHODS.>
<I'M NOT COMFORTABLE SITTING AROUND IN MY UNDERWEAR.>
<IT'S EMBARRASSING.>
<OH, I UNDERSTAND.>
<YOU DON'T WEAR BOXERS, YOU WEAR-->
<DOES IT MATTER WHAT I WEAR??>
<I'M SURE WE HAVE A PAIR OF BOXERS OR SHORTS YOU CAN BORROW.>

<HERE, THESE SHOULD FIT.>
<I PROMISE I WON'T LOOK.>
WHY DO I HAVE TO DO THIS?
LARGO'S THE ONE WHO BELIEVES ALL THIS EXCESSIVE STATIC SAFETY CRAP, NOT ME.
I SHOULD JUST TELL HER...
TELL HER THAT YOU DON'T REALLY--
<PIRO!>
<IF YOU AREN'T CHANGED IN 30 SECONDS, I'LL COME AND DO IT FOR YOU.>
<NO!! THAT'S NOT... I'M ALMOST DONE!!!>

KAPPA
TESLA STICK
chink
WKHOOM!
wap!
fwkish

<...AND WHAT IS WITH THE PINK HAIR?>
<DOES SHE THINK SHE'S AN ANIME CHARACTER?>
<YOU'RE JUST UPSET BECAUSE YANIGADA-KUN IS TALKING TO HER.>
<IT IS A LITTLE MUCH.>
<IT'S NOT PROPER. SHE STANDS OUT TOO MUCH.>
<SOMETHING NEEDS TO BE DONE.>
<AND IT'S NOT JUST HER HAIR.>
<DIDN'T YOU NOTICE?>
<YOU'RE RIGHT. WE SHOULD TALK TO HER.>
<SHE'LL NEVER FIT IN IF SHE STANDS OUT LIKE THAT.>
<IT'S FOR HER OWN GOOD.>

KERCHAK!
WHOOSH!
IT'S YOU.
YOU WANT TO TELL ME SOME-THING?
THE GUNS I NEED TO DEAL WITH YOU WILL BE HERE TOMORROW.
OR DO YOU WANNA SEE HOW EXTRA KRISPI FEELS RIGHT NOW?
I THOUGHT I MADE IT CLEAR YESTERDAY.
THESE ARE MY GAMES.
I'M NOT GOING TO LET YOU PLAY.
ANY OF YOU.

AWWW.
THAT HURTS MY...
...FEELINGS!
KRAK!
<WAS THERE AN ACCIDENT?>
EVERYONE AWAY FROM THE WINDOWS!!
<MIHO-CHAN...>
<WHAT WAS THAT?>
<DID A TRUCK HIT A POWER POLE?>
BREEEBREEEBREEEN-PROXIMITY ALERT!!-PROXIM
WHAT!?
KERPINK!

BLAM!
BLAM!
BLAM!
YOU'RE ENJOYING THIS, AREN'T YOU?
EVERYBODY BACK!! STAY AWAY FROM ALL METAL!!
<MIHO-CHAN!!!>
I DON'T CARE IF YOU ARE MADE OF PLASTIC, MOVE.
<BUT, LARGO-SENSEI! MIHO-CHAN IS, IS...>
JUST ANOTHER GRIEFER.
GRIEF THIS.
THAT ATTACK WAS ELECTRICAL IN NATURE.
IT'S DANGEROUS FOR--
ZAP!
OH NO...

WUT THE--
click click
ZAP.
WHUMP
FSHZZZZSHZZZZ
SMASH!
<KYAAA!>
WHOOM!
<AIEEE!>
WOOMP!
SMASH!
SMASH!
SMASH!
CASUALTY REPORT!!
AH... ALL STUDENTS ACCOUNTED FOR!
A FEW CUTS, SOME FIRST DEGREE BURNS, NOTHING SERIOUS.
ALL THE COMPUTERS WERE--
AH!

<UWAH!!>
<PING-SAN!! ARE YOU OK?>
<YOUR HEAD HIT THE FLOOR, I'M SORRY!>
<UEH...>
-SNIFF!-
<UEH...>
<ARE YOU HURT?>
<PING-SAN?>
<WAAAHHHH!!>
-SNIFF!-
<UNGYU...>
<WAAAHHHHAAAAAAA!!>
-SNIFF!-
-SNIFF!-
WHY ARE YOU CRYING?
-SNIFF!-
<W... WHAT?>
<WHY ARE YOU CRYING? ARE YOU HURT?>
-SNIFF!-
-SNIFF!-
<I... I... DON'T KNOW!!>
-SNIFF!-
-SNIFF!-
SHFFF.
<IT... IT... JUST STARTED AND I C... C... CAN'T-->
QUIET.
CHIRP
CHIRP
CHIRP
CHIRP
<WHAT'S SENSEI DOING?>

<...BUT LARGO SAID THESE SETTINGS WOULD WORK.>
<YEAH, BUT SETTINGS CAN CHANGE FOR UNSUPPORTED FEATURES LIKE THIS.>
<WONDER-FUL.>
<SO HOW DO WE FIGURE OUT THE NEW SETTINGS?>
<USUALLY, SOME-ONE IN THE KNOW WILL POST THEM ONLINE SOME-WHERE.>
<SOMEONE WITH INSIDE INFORMATION, HUH?>
<YEAH.>
<IF YOU HAD A WORKING COMPUTER I COULD TRY TO FIND IT...>
click
click
click
<SO, WOULD YOU LIKE SOME INSIDE INFORMATION ON NANASAWA?>
<WHAT??>
<YOU KNOW, LIKE WHAT HER FAVORITE COLOR IS, OR WHAT KINDS OF MOVIES SHE LIKES...>
<HOW SHE FEELS ABOUT WHAT HAPPENED LAST NIGHT.>
<OR HOW SHE FEELS ABOUT YOU IN GENERAL.>
<N... NO!>
<YOU DON'T WANT TO KNOW?>
<OF COURSE I DO!! BUT YOU TELLING ME ISN'T RIGHT!!>
<WHY NOT? MIGHT MAKE IT EASIER FOR YOU.>
<I DON'T WANT IT TO BE EASY!!>
<I WANT IT TO BE RIGHT!!>

huff
huff
<YOU KNOW I'M JUST TEASING YOU, RIGHT?>
<HAYA-SAKA-SAN...>
<IF NANA-SAWA-SAN NEVER WANTED TO SEE ME AGAIN...>
<WOULD YOU TELL ME?>
<I WOULDN'T TEASE YOU ABOUT IT.>
SKISH
KTHUMP
thump thump
thump
thump
kreee
SLAM!
AH. SHE RAN AWAY.
<WHAAA???>
<Y-Y-Y-YOU MEAN SHE REALLY WAS IN-->
PIRO...
KIMIKO WAS CAPTAIN OF OUR HIGH SCHOOL TRACK TEAM.
YOU WON'T CATCH HER BY STANDING THERE THINKING ABOUT IT.
JUST PUT SOME PANTS ON FIRST.

<ARE YOU SURE YOUR DAD IS COMING TO PICK YOU UP?>
<HE WAS PRETTY UPSET THAT I HURT MY-SELF YESTER-DAY.>
<HE'LL BE HERE.>
<I HOPE HE COMES SOON, YUKI-CHAN!! CALL ME LATER!>
<I WILL. SEE YA.>
<THAT IDIOT.>
<HE DID FORGET.>
pikku! pikku!
<NO.>
<I'M NOT CALLING HIM.>
fwuf!
<HE CAN FEEL GUILTY ABOUT MAKING ME WALK HOME.>
<B... B...BUT I NEVER...>
<STOP ACTING SO INNOCENT!!>
<YOU THINK WE CAN'T SEE RIGHT THROUGH YOUR LITTLE GAMES?>
<STOP CRYING!>
<NINAMORI, ENOUGH.>
SHFF.

<YOUR BEHAVIOR IS INAPPROPRIATE, PING-SAN.>
<BUT, BUT, I HAVEN'T DONE ANYTHING-->
<YOU HAVEN'T??>
<IT'S OBVIOUS YOU'VE STUFFED YOUR BRA.>
<WHAT? NO! THESE ARE MY REAL-->
<ARE YOU SAYING THEY JUST GREW THAT BIG OVER THE WEEKEND??>
<HOW DUMB DO YOU THINK WE ARE?>
<PING-SAN?>
<AND WHAT'S WITH THE HAIR?>
<DID YOU REALLY THINK COLORING IT HOT PINK WOULD BE ACCEPT-ABLE??>
<WH... WHY ARE THEY BEING SO MEAN TO HER?>
<BUT, BUT, THIS IS MY REAL... KYAA!!>
<DON'T LIE TO US!!>
<NINAMORI!>
<STOP!>
<...PLEASE?>

<THIS MATTER DOES NOT CONCERN YOU, UNDER-CLASSMAN.>
<S... SONODA-SAN~>
<BUT...>
<BUT I...>
<THIS IS AN EXAMPLE OF WHY YOUR BEHAVIOR IS REPREHENSIBLE, PING-SAN.>
<YOU KNOW HER?>
<THINK OF THE EXAMPLE YOU ARE SETTING FOR YOUNGER STUDENTS!>
<THAT WAS RATHER FOOLISH, IBARA.>
<I...>
<WHAT?>
<YOU SHOULDN'T DISMISS THE LITTLE UNDERCLASSMAN SO LIGHTLY.>
<A GIRL WITH MAGICAL POWERS SHOULD NEVER BE TAKEN LIGHTLY.>
<"MAGICAL POWERS?">
<I DON'T FIND THAT PARTICULARLY AMUSING, TOHYA.>
<M... MIHO-CHAN~>
<NEITHER DO I.>

<I SUGGEST YOU HEED OUR ADVICE, PING-SAN.>
<IT WOULD BE A SHAME IF YOU ENDED UP LIKE TOHYA.>
<A SAD NOBODY WITHOUT A LIFE.>
<MIHO-CHAAAAN~!!>
WAH-HAHHHH!!
<REMARKABLE, ISN'T IT?>
<HER EMOTIONS ARE SO REAL...>
<IT CAN EVEN FOOL MONSTERS LIKE YOU AND ME.>
<HNNNG~>
SNIFF! SNIFF!

<FEELING ANY BETTER, DEAR?>
<UHN.>
SNIFF!
<M...M... MONSTERS??>
<IT'S A GENERAL TERM. I'M SURE YOU'VE HEARD YOUR DAD USE IT.>
SNIFF
<YOU KNOW...>
<IF YOU TAKE AWAY THE SELF RIGHTEOUSNESS AND NEUROTIC OBSESSION WITH HELPING OTHERS, WE'RE NOT THAT DIFF-ERENT.>
<YOU FEED ON THE EMOTIONS THE SAME WAY I DO.>
<WHAT ARE YOU TALKING ABOUT??>
<TOHYA-SAN!>
<OH COME NOW, YOU REALLY HAVEN'T FIGURED IT OUT?>
<FIGURED WHAT OUT??>
<STOP SAYING WEIRD THINGS AND SPEAK PLAINLY!!>
<TOHYA-SAN!!>
<M... MIHO-CHAN??>

<MIHO-CHAN!!>
<SONODA-SAN~!!>
<PLEASE...>
<PLEASE DON'T...>
<PLEASE DON'T LEAVE ME BEHIND...>
<PING-SAN?>
<NANA-SAWA-SAN!?>
<IT IS YOU! PING-SAN, WHAT'S WRONG?>
<LARGO-SENSEI SAID HE KNEW WHAT'S WRONG WITH ME BUT WOULDN'T TELL ME AND THEN CLASS ENDED AND AFTER SCHOOL I TRIED TO FIND HIM BUT THE GIRLS FROM CLASS GOT MAD AT ME AND YELLED AT ME AND AND-->
<WOAH, PING-SAN, CALM DOWN, IT'S OK.>
<I'M TRYING SO HARD BUT THINGS KEEP BLOWING UP AND EVERYONE IS YELLING AT ME AND MY FRIENDS ARE RUNNING AWAY FROM ME AND I CAN'T STOP CRYING...>
<I DON'T KNOW WHAT'S WRONG WITH ME!!>
<SHHH, DON'T CRY SWEETIE.>
<I DON'T THINK ANYONE EVER KNOWS.>
WAAHHH!!

SNIFF
<YOU THINK THERE'S SOMETHING WRONG WITH YOU TOO?>
<THERE'S PROBABLY SOMETHING WRONG WITH EVERY-ONE, PING-SAN.>
SNIFF SNIFF
<SOME OF US ARE JUST A LITTLE MORE SCREWED UP THAN OTHERS.>
<BUT... PIRO-SAN CHOSE **YOU**, NANASAWA-SAN! HE WOULDN'T DO THAT IF THERE WAS ANYTHING WRONG WITH YOU!>
<UWAHH!! I'M SORRY! I SHOULDN'T HAVE GIVEN YOU THAT DATA! I'M NOT THE ONE WHO-->
<NO, NO, PING-SAN, IT'S OK!>
<I...>
<I KNOW.>
<YOU DO? **WAI!!** CONGRATULATIONS!!>
<DID HE TELL YOU? DID HE CONFESS HIS LOVE? DID HE...>
<NANA-SAWA-SAN?>

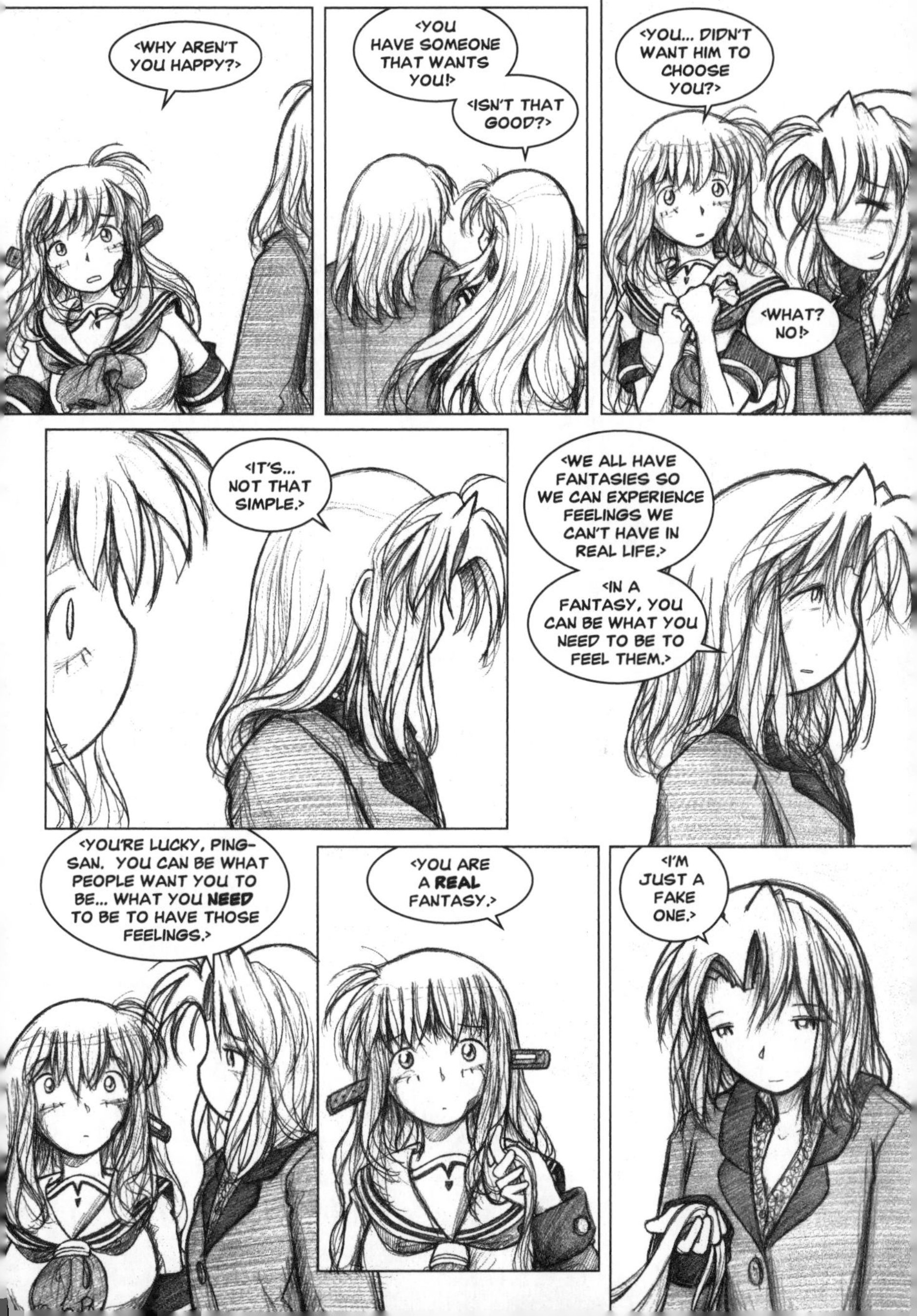

<WHY AREN'T YOU HAPPY?>
<YOU HAVE SOMEONE THAT WANTS YOU!>
<ISN'T THAT GOOD?>
<YOU... DIDN'T WANT HIM TO CHOOSE YOU?>
<WHAT? NO!>
<IT'S... NOT THAT SIMPLE.>
<WE ALL HAVE FANTASIES SO WE CAN EXPERIENCE FEELINGS WE CAN'T HAVE IN REAL LIFE.>
<IN A FANTASY, YOU CAN BE WHAT YOU NEED TO BE TO FEEL THEM.>
<YOU'RE LUCKY, PING-SAN. YOU CAN BE WHAT PEOPLE WANT YOU TO BE... WHAT YOU **NEED** TO BE TO HAVE THOSE FEELINGS.>
<YOU ARE A **REAL** FANTASY.>
<I'M JUST A FAKE ONE.>

<BUT... I DON'T WANT TO BE A FANTASY.>
<NANA-SAWA-SAN?>
<I DON'T THINK... I WANT TO BE ONE EITHER.>
<GOOD THING, TOO. I SUCK AT IT.>
<HOW CAN I STOP BEING A FANTA-SY?>
<WELL...>
<START LOOKING PAST THE FEELINGS YOU **THINK** YOU WANT TO HAVE...>
<AND FIND THE ONES YOU **REALLY** CARE ABOUT.>
JR
JR

<STOP TEASING ME! I'M NOT A CHILD!!>
<TOHYA-SAN!!>
<I'M NOT A "MAGICAL GIRL" JUST BECAUSE I TRIED TO HELP SOMEONE!!>
<AND YOU'RE NOT A MONSTER! STOP SAYING THINGS LIKE THAT!!>
<TOHYA-SAN, STOP AND LISTEN TO ME!!>
<STOP?>
<ARE YOU SURE YOU WANT TO STOP HERE?>
<I FIND BALANCING ON POWER LINES TO BE A LITTLE DISQUIETING.>
<MIND IF I STAND HERE?>

<UWAEHH!!>
<U...>
<U...>
<UWAH!>
WHAK!
<RELAX, YUKI.>
<EEE!>
FWWOOOOOWWWN!!
<NO ONE WILL SEE.>
<THEY ARE AS AFRAID TO LOOK UP AS WE ARE TO LOOK DOWN.>
<WHAT WAS THAT?>
<HUH.>
<OH WELL.>

<I... I DON'T UNDER-STAND! WHA... WHAT-->
<MANY GIRLS FANTASIZE ABOUT BEING A "MAGICAL GIRL" WHEN THEY ARE YOUNG.>
<YOU DON'T HAVE TO.>
<YOU ARE ONE.>
<EXCITING, ISN'T IT?>
<YOU CAN BE THE FOCUS OF EVERYONE'S LOVE AND ATTENTION JUST BY BEING YOURSELF.>
<YOU'RE NOT JUST ANOTHER LITTLE GIRL WHO ISN'T REALLY THAT IMPORT-ANT.>
<T... TOHYA-SAN?>
<I DON'T BLAME YOU FOR BEING A LITTLE SCARED.>
<SUCH DRASTIC SHIFTS IN YOUR REALITY ARE NEVER EASY.>
<MOST PEOPLE NEVER HAVE THEM.>
<BE HAPPY YOURS HAS BEEN A GOOD ONE.>

<TOHYA-SAN?>
<ARE YOU SAYING...>
<YOURS WAS REALLY BAD?>
<TOHYA-SAN!!>

<K...K... KOBAYASHI-KUN?!?>
<N... NO, PLEASE! DON'T LOO-->
<--UWAH!>
<A...>
<AH...!>
AIEEEEEEEE!

<NANA-SAWA-SAN?>
<THEY'RE JUST CARDBOARD, THEY AREN'T REAL.>
SHFFFF!
HEL-LO~!
YO.
YOU BROUGHT THE ROBOT. GOOD.
<GOOD AFTERNOON, LARGO-SAN! HOW ARE YOU? THANK YOU FOR WHAT YOU DID FOR ME THE OTHER NIGHT!>
<WOW, LOOK AT ALL THE BOXES! I'M SURE YOU GUYS ARE BUSY, I JUST STOPPED IN TO SAY HI. IS PIRO-SAN HERE?>
<IF HE'S NOT BUSY, THAT IS.>
<AH, ER... LARGO-SAN! YOUR HAIR! YOUR FACE! WHAT HAPPENED? DID... DID...>
KONNICHI-WA, LARGO-SENSEI.
<UH, PING-SAN...>
<HELP!>
<IT'S OK! LARGO-SENSEI ISN'T HURT. NO ONE WAS HURT BAD WHEN THE CLASSROOM BLEW UP.>

<WHA? NO, I... I CAN'T SPEAK ENGLISH, CAN-->
<NEITHER CAN PING.>
<YOU CAN'T?>
<I... I'LL GO SEE IF I CAN FIND PIRO-SAN.>
<OK.>
<WHY IS SHE SO NERVOUS ABOUT TALKING TO PIRO-SAN?>
<WAH?>
IT IS AS I PH33R'D.
CHIRP!
LARGO...
<UWAH!>
WHENEVER YOU SAY THAT I END UP HAVING TO HUNT FOR FIRE EXTINGUISHERS WE HAVEN'T USED UP YET.
PLEASE TELL ME PING ISN'T ABOUT TO BURST INTO FLAMES.

IS BURSTING INTO FLAMES THE USUAL FAILURE MODE FOR ONE OF THESE?
NO, BUT IT'S THE USUAL FAILURE MODE FOR ANYTHING YOU TOUCH.
YOU UNDERSTAND THIS CR4P.
EXPLAIN TO ME WHAT I AM DOING WRONG.
THESE EDS UNITS HAVE AN "EMOTIONAL" OPERATING SYSTEM.
EMOSHUNARU...?
ALL OF ITS LOGICAL OPERATIONS ARE SUBJECT TO A MULTITUDE OF "EMOTIONAL" MODIFIERS.
<K... KIMIKO-SAN!?>
<IS LARGO-SENSEI TALKING ABOUT ME?>
GENERALLY, THESE MODIFIERS ARE SELF BALANCING.
<HE SAID HE KNEW WHAT WAS WRONG WITH ME! IS HE TELLING YOU??>
BUT IF THE BALANCE ISN'T MAINTAINED, THE SYSTEM WILL BEHAVE ERRATICALLY.
<PIRO-SAN! PLEASE TELL ME!! WHAT IS HE SAYING!?!>
<TELL HER, PIRO-SAN.>
WHEN THIS HAPPENS, AN "EMOTIONAL PURGE" UTILITY WILL RUN TO FIX THE ERRORS.
<IT'S IMPORTANT TO HER.>

<...WHEN THE STATIC DISCHARGE CAUSED THE CLASSROOM TO EXPLODE, YOU FAINTED.>
<WHEN YOU WOKE UP, YOU STARTED CRYING.>
<THAT WAS YOUR "EMOTIONAL PURGE" UTILITY RUNNING. YOU FELT CONFUSED, OVER-WHELMED, AND COULDN'T STOP CRYING.>
<BUT THE CRYING STOPPED, RIGHT?>
<FEEL BETTER?>
<OH! UH... YEAH. IT DID.>
<A LITTLE.>
<SEE? IT WORKED.>
<LARGO'S JUST CONCERNED BECAUSE IT DIDN'T FIX **ALL** OF THE ERRORS.>
<THE LEAKED BETA RELEASE DOCUMENTATION SAYS IT'S SUPPOSED TO.>
<WEHH?? I HAVE ERRORS IT COULDN'T FIX??>
<AM I BROKEN??>
<WHAT? NO! IT'S ONLY A FEW ERROR CODES. EVERY-THING ELSE IS FINE, RIGHT?>
<EVERYONE HAS **SOME** ERRORS, PING. IT DOESN'T MEAN WE'RE BROKEN.>
<IT'S PART OF WHAT MAKES US...>
<US...>
DON'T TELL IT TOO MUCH. IT MIGHT GO INTO A B3RZ3RKER R4MP4G3 AND KILL US ALL.
HUH?

<SO... YOU REALLY THINK...>
<I'M OK?>
<THE ERRORS ARE ALL BEING CAUSED BY CONFLICTING EMOTIONAL MODIFIERS.>
<AS LONG AS YOUR SYSTEM CAN MANAGE THEM AND COMPENSATE FOR THEM YOU SHOULD BE FINE.>
<I THINK SO.>
<OPERATION-ALLY YOU'RE FINE.>
<SO... I'M...OK.>
IS THIS W33P RESPONSE A REACTION TO YOU INFORMING IT OF ITS IMPENDING SHUTDOWN?
LARGO, I TOLD YOU, WE CAN'T TURN HER OFF.
DIDN'T YOU READ ANY OF THAT MANUAL?
IS THAT A SERIOUS QUESTION?
SHE'S DESIGNED TO BE LIKE A REAL GIRL.
YOU CAN'T SHUT THEM OFF WHILE YOU FIGURE OUT WHAT TO DO.
THAT'S WHY HER ERROR CORRECTION ROUTINES ARE SO ROBUST.
<UHM, PIRO-SAN?>
<DIDN'T ERIKA WANT LARGO-SAN TO CALL HER?>
<ABOUT THAT... COM-PUTER?>
<EH?>
OH! RIGHT! ERIKA'S COMPUTER! IT... WON'T WORK. THERE'S SOME WEIRD JUMPER SET--
WAS IT ASSEMBLED PROPERLY?
YEAH! I WENT OVER AND DID WHAT I COULD TO--
WAS SHE N4K3D?
NO!!

YO.
PIRO TELLS ME THE SYSTEM WON'T BOOT.
THERE ARE SEVERAL THINGS YOU NEED TO--
<I THINK I'LL GO UPSTAIRS AND CHANGE.>
WHAT?
YES, I FILLED IN FOR YOU TODAY.
<OH! ARE YOU OK NOW, PING?>
I HAD TO LEAVE TO TEACH MY CLASS.
<UH HUH! THANK YOU, PIRO-SAN!>
<YOU TOO, NANASAWA-SAN!>
I AM A TEACHER AT THE LOCAL HIGH SCHOOL.
<UHM... HEY.>
<HELLO.>
I DO NOT UNDERSTAND WHY YOU ARE LAUGHING.

WE MUST GET YOUR SYSTEM WORKING. IT HAS BEEN INACTIVE FOR TOO LONG.
<I...>
<UHM.>
tak--tak-tak tak--tak
FWISH! FWISH!
AAAAAGHH!
TRY THESE JUMPER SETTINGS...
<I'M... I'M SORRY.>
<I'M TOO TIRED...>
<TO MAKE WHAT I WANT TO SAY...>
<COME OUT RIGHT.>
THAT WORKED?
3XC3LL3NT! WE MUST TEST IT! I WILL GO UPSTAIRS AND--
WHAT? YOU WANT ME TO COME THERE TO TEST IT?

WE'RE GOING TO DINNER AT THE SONODAS', REMEMBER?
YOU CAN TEST THIS THING BEFORE WE GO.
DINNER? WITH THAT COP?
IT WAS VERY NICE OF THAT "COP" AND HIS WIFE TO INVITE US TO DINNER.
DON'T BE A JERK.
UGHHH...
OH, COME ON, IT WON'T BE--
THEY'RE HUGGING.
HUGGING?
WHO'S HUGGING?
PIRO AND YOUR ROOM-MATE.
REALLY.
IT IS IMPOSSIBLE TO TEST A L33T SYSTEM WITHOUT SUBJECTING IT TO A MASSIV3 LIV3 FIR3 FR4GF357.
THIS CANNOT BE DONE WITH A SINGLE MACHINE. I MUST ENGAGE YOU FROM MY SYSTEM HERE.
I WILL GIVE YOU INFORMATION ON WHAT SERVER TO LOG--
LARGO...
SHUT UP AND GET OVER HERE.

bwep.
SIGH
<IDIOT.>
SNAP!
bwep.
bwep.
bwep.
<MEIMI-SAN?>
<THIS IS ERIKA. HOW ARE YOU?>
<I'M OK. YES, WE'RE FINE.>
<I'M REALLY SORRY, BUT LARGO AND I WON'T BE ABLE TO MAKE IT TO DINNER TONIGHT. CAN WE-->
<TOMORROW? SURE, THAT'D BE GREAT.>

<I'M SORRY, I'M SO SORRY.>
<NO, DON'T BE.>
<IT'S, IT'S...>
PIRO.
UWAH!
SHE IS INSISTING THAT I TRAVEL TO HER LOCATION TO TEST HER COMPUTER BUILD.
I EXPLAINED TO HER THAT I CANNOT SH4K3-DWN HER BOX THERE.
<UHM, AH...>
WHAT?
I NEED AN ADDITIONAL SYSTEM TO PROPERLY TEST THE BUILD.
SHE UNDER-STANDS THIS.
AH...
YET SHE STILL INSISTS THAT I COME.
<HI! CAN... CAN I HELP YOU?>
DUDE.
I MAY NOT BE ABLE TO DO WHAT I NEED TO DO IF I GO.
WHAT SHOULD I DO?

WHAT SHOULD YOU DO?
SHE WANTS TO SEE YOU, YOU IDIOT! GO!!
DUDE, I PH33R IT IS NOT WIZ3 TO GO IN WITHOUT SUFFICIENT...
DOU KA SHIMASHITA?
AI NI KOI TTE HAYASAKA-SAN NI IWARETEMASHITA KEDO, KOITSU WA BAKA NAN DESU!
LARGO
ERIKA KYOU ZUTTO LARGO-SAN NI AITAKATTANO DESU.
MATTEIMASU YO.
ITTE AGETA HOU GA II TO OMOIMASU.
I MUST... PREPARE FOR THE JOURNEY.
NAN...
HUH.
HOW DID YOU DO THAT?
NANA-SAWA-SAMA.
WAH!
<ON BEHALF OF EVERYONE YOU GRACED LAST NIGHT WITH THE HONOR OF YOUR SERVICE...>
<I HUMBLY PRESENT MY SINCEREST AND DEEPEST APOLOGIES FOR OUR BEHA-VIOR.>

<REHH? UH, PLEASE, YOU DON'T HAVE TO-->
<Y-YES I DO!!>
<THE WAY YOU CONFRONTED US ABOUT HOW BAD OUR INSENSITIVE ACTIONS WERE MAKING YOU FEEL. THE WAY WE RESPONDED TO YOUR CHALLENGE...>
<WE FAILED YOU.>
<I... MANY OF US... HAVE NEVER FELT SO ASHAMED.>
<THERE ARE LOTS OF ARGUMENTS NOW, MANY WHO SAY WE SHOULDN'T BE ASHAMED, THAT IT IS YOUR JOB TO BE OUR FANTASY.>
<I...>
<BUT MANY OF US FEEL WE MUST RISE TO YOUR CHALLENGE AND RESPECT YOUR FEELINGS, EVEN IF IT MEANS WE HAVE TO SACRIFICE OUR OWN FANTASIES!>
<WE WILL FIGHT TO PROTECT YOUR FEELINGS THE SAME WAY YOU PROTECTED OURS, NANASAWA-SAN!!>
<AH! WAIT!>
SHFFF!
<WOAH.>
FWUFF!
<YOU DO REALIZE THAT MAKIN' OUT IN FRONT OF THEM KINDA FREAKS 'EM OUT.>
<EHH WHA?>

KNOCK KNO
<AH.>
SO, WHAT TOOK YOU SO--
...LONG.
THE WEIGHT OF MY EQUIPMENT REDUCED THE PERFORMANCE OF THE MUFFIN CART.
I WAS UNABLE TO DRIVE FAST.
HOW MUCH EQUIPMENT DID YOU BRING?
AND WHAT HAPPENED TO YOUR FACE?
YOU LOOK LIKE YOU'VE BEEN...
IS THIS A SYNTHETIC FABRIC?!?
WHA?
Y-YES, IT'S A SWIM--
SYNTHETIC FABRICS GENERATE TREMENDOUS AMOUNTS OF STATIC ELEC-TRICITY!!
THE DISCHARGE CAUSED BY THIS COULD DETONATE A SYSTEM AS L33T AS YOURS!
THIS OUTFIT IS DANGER-OUS!!
YOU WANT ME TO TAKE IT OFF?

WHAT, NOW YOU **DON'T** WANT ME TO GET NAKED?
NO.
IT WOULD... DISTRACT ME.
SO, ME NAKED MIGHT DISTRACT YOU, BUT ME IN A BIKINI DOESN'T BOTHER YOU.
OF COURSE IT BOTHERS ME!!
YOU... BOTHER ME.
YOU PUT A LOT OF EFFORT INTO THIS.
I DON'T WANT TO DISRESPECT YOUR WORK BY BEING...
DISTRACTED...
BY YOU.
STILL, THAT FABRIC IS DANGER-OUS.
YOU CAN CHANGE INTO SOMETHING NATURAL WHILE I RETRIEVE THE REST OF MY EQUIPMENT.
SO, BY "NATURAL," DO YOU MEAN "NAKED"?
NATURAL FABRIC! NATURAL FABRIC!!!

<WHAT A DAY.>
<I REALLY THOUGHT WE WERE GONNA HAVE AN ARMY OF YOUR FANS DESCENDING ON THE STORE AFTER THAT ONE GUY LEFT.>
<SO RELIEVED WE DIDN'T HAVE TO DEAL WITH ANOTHER FANBOY RIOT.>
<THEY SEEM TO DO THAT A LOT AROUND HERE.>
<NOT REALLY. HEH.>
<I DON'T BLAME YOU FOR WANTING TO GET TAKE OUT.>
<THAT'S GONNA SUCK, ALWAYS BEING AFRAID TO SHOW YOUR FACE IN PUBLIC JUST BECAUSE SOME IDIOTS CAN'T CONTROL THEMSELVES.>
<UGH. I'M SO TIRED...>
<I'M SORRY.>
<I'M SURE IT WON'T BE THAT BAD.>
<OH, NO, I'M SURE IT WON'T BE.>
PAT
<IT'LL BE OK.>
<YOU DON'T HAVE TO DEAL WITH IT BY YOURSELF, KIMIKO-SAN.>

<KIMIKO-SAN, WHAT'S WRONG?>
<IS IT SOMETHING I-->
<PIRO-SAN, PLEASE...>
<IT'S NOT YOU.>
<PLEASE, I... I DON'T WANT YOU TO WORRY ABOUT IT.>
<THE HELL I'M NOT GONNA WORRY ABOUT IT!!>
<I MEAN...>
<IT'S JUST...>
<I MEAN...>
FUMP!
<Y'CAN TELL ME NOT TO WORRY ALL Y'WANT.>
<BUT I'M STILL GONNA.>
shfff...
FUFF
<LATE NIGHT TV IS TERRIBLE, ISN'T IT?>
<YEAH...>
<IT IS.>

NO\/\/!!
MOV3! MOV3! MOV3!!
PING!
WATCH IT MISTER, OR I'LL HAUL--
THPFT!
CRAK
GAH!
H4UL 17, WOMAN!!
USOU~!!
FSCK!!!
WE'RE NEVER GONNA GET PAST THIS SPOT.
YOU SAID THAT AT THE FLESH AEROSOL-ER.
WE PWNZED THAT.
YEAH, EVENTUAL-LY.
I THINK YOU SHOULD GO ON WITHOUT ME.
WHAT?
YOU HEARD ME. I'M HOLDING YOU BACK.
MY MACHINE WORKS FINE, YOU SHOULDN'T HAVE TO SUFFER BEING PINNED DOWN HERE BY--
NO.
I CAME HERE TO PLAY WITH YOU.
NOT SOME LAME CAMPER WITH A SNIPER RIG.

REALLY?
OF COURSE.
CAN WE PLAY ONE OF MY GAMES?
SURE.
FIRST LEMME SEE IF I CAN CAP THIS SNIPER.
FSHHHIP
JUST... ONE SHOT.
A CLEAN SHOT, THAT'S ALL I NEED...
THAT'S...

TSK, TSK, TSK...
CLIK CLIK
I THINK SOMEONE IS DISTRACTED.
THPUNK!
YOU SHOULDN'T BRING THINGS TO THIS WORLD THAT DISTRACT YOU, LARGO.
CHIK CLIK
ESPECIALLY DANGEROUS THINGS...
...LIKE YOU.
HE DOESN'T UNDERSTAND WHAT YOU CAN DO TO THIS WORLD.
HOW MUCH MORE POWERFUL YOU CAN BE BY BEING HERE.
THPUNK!
AND HOW IT MAKES YOU THAT MUCH MORE...
VALUABLE.

<PIRO-SAN? NANASAWA-SAN?>
<CAN I COME UP?>
<G'NIGHT, PIRO-SAN, NANASAWA-SAN.>

KERCHACK
squeeee
YO, PIRO...
SKSHHHH
FUMP.
END CHAPTER 8

megatokyo "Leave it to Seraphim!"
OUR READERS ARE VERY IMPORTANT TO US. WITHOUT YOU, WE'D BE OUT OF A JOB.
SO IN TODAY'S EPISODE OF "LEAVE IT TO SERAPHIM" I WANT TO TALK ABOUT SOMETHING VERY IMPORTANT...
YOUR HEALTH!
AT THE RATE THIS GUY IS DOING THE COMIC, IT IS NECESSARY THAT YOU LIVE AS LONG AS POSSIBLE SO YOU CAN SEE THE FINAL EPISODES.
HEY.
MY RESEARCH SHOWS THAT MOST OF YOU ARE NOT AS HEALTHY AS YOU COULD BE.
HERE ARE SOME SIMPLE THINGS YOU CAN DO TO CHANGE THIS!
FIRST OFF, GET AWAY FROM THAT COMPUTER!! GO OUTSIDE! MOVE AROUND! EXERCISE!!
THE SUN IS NOT EVIL!
DISCOVER PARTS OF YOUR BODY YOU FORGOT EXISTED, LIKE YOUR FEET!
DON'T ESCAPE INTO YOUR TV, ESCAPE OUTSIDE!!
OH, BE SURE TO WEAR LOTS OF SUNSCREEN.
EAT HEALTHY!
LEARN WHAT A FRUIT IS!
TOFU IS THE OTHER, OTHER WHITE MEAT!
CORN AND POTATO CHIPS DO NOT COUNT AS VEGETABLES!
I KNOW IT'S HARD, BUT IT WILL BE WORTH IT TO BE AROUND WHEN PIRO FINALLY FINISHES THE STORY!
I THINK YOU WORRY TOO MUCH. I'M SURE MOST OF OUR READERS HAVE THE SAME EATING AND EXERCISE HABITS I HAVE.
LOOK AT ME, I'M OK.
CRINKLE
CRUNCH
CRUNCH
CRUNCH
HEY.

Shirt_Guy_Dom.txt

Back when I started *Megatokyo,* there was one thing I wanted to avoid: fan abuse.

Fan abuse is what happens when a malicious creator crafts characters that we all care about and then proceeds to abuse them in ways that are painful for fans to watch or read. *Evangelion* is a prime example of this. There is nothing wrong with having tension in a story, or making fans worry about a favorite character, but when it goes too far I have a problem with it.

I like to think that I've done a pretty good job of avoiding fan abuse. I don't think there are too many readers who have been traumatized by anything I've done with the story. It's nice to think that when people come to *Megatokyo* they don't have to worry about being traumatized in any way by...

Oh. Oh yeah. "Shirt Guy Dom" strips. Forgot about those.

"Shirt Guy Dom" strips are what happen when I let Dom loose on the helpless *Megatokyo* horde with his disturbingly demonic trackball art and soul-destroying stick fetish. Why do I do let him do this? I don't know. Maybe it's my way of making sure readers appreciate even my worst artwork. Maybe it's a kind of release, a proxy for all the fan abuse I secretly wish I could do myself...

Uhm, no, I don't want to look too close at that.

Remember, if they really bother you, you can always tear out the next two pages. I'm sure he won't hurt you if you do that. At least, I don't think he would.

I KNOW WHERE YOU LIVE.
tak tak tak
tak tak tak

SPECIAL "KNIGHTS OF THE DINNER TABLE" SGD STRIP

STICK FIGURES & PAIN: DOMINIC NGUYEN

STICK FIGURES & SPEARS: DOMINIC NGUYEN

March 13, 2006
Palo Alto, CA
First day of the job. I have a cubicle now--it's been a while since I had one. My back is to everyone passing through the hall and a couple of office doors, though, and that makes me nervous.
How nerdy is that, huh? Like a ninja is going to burst out behind me and attack or something. Oh well, I'll live. Just have to stay calm and not panic.
March 15
Maria from HR came up behind me a minute ago to ask if my phone was set up yet. Scared the hell out of me. I really need a wall or something, this is getting pretty damn annoying.
March 17
Tried turning my desk around today to ease the paranoia. Now I can't get out. This is no better than before. Gotta figure out a better solution this weekend.
March 20
I've brought couch cushions from home and built a fort behind me.
It's not helping. I still jump every time someone walks behind me. The girls in the office think it's funny. I don't see the humor in it.
March 22
Some executives from Germany came for a meeting in the office behind me today. German sounds so threatening, I kept twitching whenever they started talking. For all I know, they could've been talking about the weather.
Or plotting my demise.
March 24
IT is out to get me. I know it. I'll get them first, though. I've constructed a crude spear out of the potted plant down the hall.
I have to be vigilant. I have to--
DOM?
INCOMING!
HEY, I JUST WANTED TO SEE IF YOU WERE FREE FOR A LITTLE PROJ--DOM?
YOU'LL NEVER TAKE ME!
SNARL
(DOM'S BOSS)
GOD, MY SPLEEN! WHY IS IT ALWAYS THE SPLEEN?!
Plus: I don't feel as nervous about people coming up behind me anymore.
Minus: I think I'm fired.

FLIGHT RISK - DOMINIC NGUYEN

STICK FIGURES & FETISHISTIC LUGGAGE CONTENTS: DOMINIC NGUYEN

Dead_Piro_Art_Days.txt

"Dead Piro Days" are days when i am not able to produce a comic because I'm sick, behind schedule, busy with other projects, or just wanting to do something different. They have become known as "Dead Piro Art Days" because i usually post a drawing or sketch that is often of higher quality than the drawings i typically create for the comics themselves. I had quite a lot of DPDs to choose from for this book, and some of them aren't too bad.

The Sonoda Yuki image on page 210 was done for a clearfile poster and the PoleSitting image on page 211 is was for a poster that Hawk and I worked on in August 2006. It was difficult to create a Japanese looking pole for Miho to sit on. Different wiring, different insulators, different support structures, different transformers... the overhead wiring in Japan is woven into different patterns than the overhead wiring here in the States.

My favorite two sketches in this book are on page 212 and 213. The sketch of Ping walking away from Yuki who is waiting for her dad to pick her up is almost like a missing scene from the story. The sketch of Kimiko walking across the porch of a decrepit house is something I did for Halloween and has an oddly spooky feel to it that I find appealing.

The Ph33r The Cute Ones drawings on pages 216 and 217 are attempts to re-create the feel of a drawing I did years ago that inspired the idea for Piroko. I actually prefer 216 over 217 for some reason, even though the latter one is a better drawing. It's just much more dramatic, I guess.

As for the Christmas images on pages 218 and 219...219 is very cute (doing a largo snowman was pretty challenging) but there is something really wrong with Piroko in reindeer drag, never mind Largo as Santa. >_<

Well, that's what DPDs are all about. They are a chance to experiment and show things I haven't been able to show in the story, or show things that have nothing to do with the story. It is their random nature that makes them an interesting by-product of the creative process.

YANRDPD (yet another not really dead piro day)

CHARACTER SNAPSHOT: S|<OO|_ D4YZ

I WAS WORKING ON THE NEXT COMIC AND FOUND MYSELF SKETCHING THIS. AFTER A WHILE, I LOOKED AT THE DRAWINGS FOR THE COMIC, LOOKED AT THIS, AND DECIDED I LIKED IT MUCH BETTER :) YAY FOR RANDOMNESS :P KIMIKO AND ERIKA FROM THEIR HIGH SCHOOL DAYS... MAYBE... (NO IDEA WHO IS IN THE BACKGROUND HERE...)

園田由紀
sonoda yuki

pol3sitting

WHEN PUTTING THE "POLESITTING" POSTER TOGETHER, MUCH OF THIS DRAWING WAS CROPPED OUT FOR THE FINAL PRINT. THIS SHOWS THE ENTIRE DRAWING, INCLUDING A RATHER COMPLICATED RENDITION OF A JAPANESE POWER POLE.

TPCD 6H74

A SLIGHTLY MORE SERIOUS LARGO DPD. (YES, I KNOW THERE ARE SERIOUS TACTICAL SNAFUS HERE, SO DON'T JUMP ON ME ABOUT THEM. IT'S A RANDOM SKETCH, SO SUE ME.)

PIRO

endgames
LARGO
legionnaire of reaht

B4K4.MD3 RELOAD WITH A HIGHER GRAPHITE COUNT
ph34r t3h cut3 on3s
r 3 d u ><

such the cute little bandaids
megatokyo : in service day

i've tripped up some of the event sequences at the tail end of this chapter and i need to fix them.

this art is actually from a revival of the classic ph34r t3h cute ones t-shirt.

-piro-

(this one of several images i did for Christmas 2006, the one on the next page is the one we chose to color and post on christmas day.)

Happy Holidays

Happy Holidays, Merry Christmas and best wishes for a Happy New Year from everyone here at MegatoKyo.com!

gameworlds : vacation

Two_Weeks-DPD_set.txt

It's rare for me to sell drawings. I never do commissions because I really can't draw other people's ideas, and the drawings I create on my own are, in my opinion, not really worth much more than the paper they are drawn on.

That said, on those rare occasions where I have put up a drawing or two for auction (usually for server upgrades or to raise money for charity) the response has always been surprising, leaving me feeling more than a little guilty about the price paid by the winning bidder. I hate feeling guilty, so aside from charity auctions at conventions, the sale of my work still tends to be rather rare.

These drawings are from a series of four DPDs that I auctioned off last year to raise funds to do something special I wanted to do for Sarah. I won't say what they sold for (you can browse the website if you are curious, I think I mentioned it in a rant), but let's just say it was far more than I needed, and I still feel guilty about it.

These drawings are essentially reflections of the "Circuity" short story I was working on for *Megatokyo* volume 4. If you are wondering what it is with me and this "girls with wings" meme, I'm not really sure either.

There's something about these drawings I find particularly haunting...having wings that don't work, wings that can be caught by the wind, carrying you away... Damaged wings, full wings, small wings, no wings at all...

Guilt aside, maybe there is something in these that makes them worth a little more than the paper I drew them on. Just a little.

tak
tak
tak
tak
tak
tak

two weeks

drawing #1 : broken blades

two weeks

drawing #2 : tilting windmills

two weeks

drawing #3 : movement of air

two weeks

drawing #4 : stillness

Readers_guide_intro.txt

One thing that *Megatokyo* has needed for a long time is a decent Readers Guide. If you are a regular reader, you are probably familiar with the "I'll finish this section when i feel like it" notices where the "Story" and "Character" pages should be. Most people think I have an attitude problem, I'm lazy or I've been too busy to work on it. The latter is the most correct, though there are other reasons why the Story and Character pages have gone unfinished for so long.

I once did an interview where I was asked to sum up Megatokyo in a few sentences. After struggling with this for about ten minutes I realized I couldn't do it. *Megatokyo* has been such a nebulous project that I'm frequently amazed how well it has come together. The only successful way I've found of communicating the story has been to create it. Summarizing requires me to give importance to some story elements while ignoring others. Since the main theme of *Megatokyo* is how everyone has different perceptions of the world around them, I've been wary of giving any "official" takes outside of the story because I don't want to color readers' perceptions. Character guides need to be updated on a regular basis because characters change and grow. It's easier to tell people to just read the comic.

With Eight chapters, five books and almost 1000 pages of material, it's getting to the point that telling people to 'read the comic' is a little unfair. There are a number of fan-run websites that have excellent story and character guides and I often direct people to them, but it is time for an official one.

If you are new to Megatokyo and this is the first book you've read, I hope that this guide helps get you up to date with the story and perhaps better understand what is going on. Since there are often many details in a story like this that no synopsis or sound bite can adequately cover, I still recommend you start at the beginning and read it through. It's far more entertaining than any synopsis could ever be. :)

tak
tak
tak
tak
tak
tak

What is Megatokyo?

Megatokyo is the story of two American gamers who find themselves stuck in Tokyo, Japan, unable to afford tickets home. The people they meet and the experiences they have are colored by their unique and contrasting perceptions of Tokyo and the world around them. These include familiar elements from a variety of anime/manga genres: Schoolgirls, ninjas, robots, giant monsters, magical girls, idol singers, gun toting enforcers, love, sadness, life philosophy from video games, and the looming threat of zombie hordes, just to name a few.

Begun in 2000 by artist/writer Fred Gallagher and co-writer Rodney Caston (who left the project in 2002) Megatokyo has become one of the most well known comics on the internet, as well has having a highly successful run of print volumes. New comic pages are published online three times a week on Monday, Wednesday, and Friday at **www.megatokyo.com.**

The Story

Chapter 0: Relax, We Understand J00 *published in: Megatokyo Volume 1*

Piro and Largo, two American gamers, travel to Tokyo on a whim and find they can't afford tickets home. They hook up with Piro's friend Tsubasa and move in with him. On an excursion into the city, Piro is confronted about his choice of reading material by a young schoolgirl named Sonoda Yuki. After Piro flees the scene, Yuki finds Piro's bookbag — and his sketchbook. Depressed about his failure to find his lost bookbag, Piro helps out a young woman named Nanasawa Kimiko who doesn't have enough money to buy a rail card and walks off before she can thank him. Piro lands a job at the MegaGamers store when a woman named Hayasaka Erika (who happens to be Kimiko's friend and roommate) abruptly hires him. Piro's conscience Seraphim, who is trying to help Piro work through his problems, is sent an assistant to take charge of Largo - a hamster named Boo. Largo runs into a spooky young woman named Tohya Miho, senses evil in her, and reacts accordingly. Tsubasa introduces Piro to Ping, a prototype robot girl and console accessory for dating simulation games. After being convinced by Ping to search for his childhood love, Tsubasa suddenly departs for America, leaving Piro and Largo no place to stay and Ping to take care of.

Chapter 1: Do You Want To Save Before You Quit? *published in: Megatokyo Volume 2*

While trying to track down t3h 3vil girl from yesterday, Largo finds himself hired as an English teacher for her class. Ping also joins the class, and is immediately befriended by Miho, who notices that she is a game accessory. A nervous Yuki returns Piro's bookbag to him at MegaGamers, and yells at Piro for not thinking his artwork is any good. After school Largo meets Miho and Ping at a local arcade where a massive showdown ends in a draw. Piro arrives in the aftermath, and Miho realizes that she knows him. Kimiko, who had recognized Piro in the store the day before while visiting Erika, decides to bring dinner to Piro at his new home in the apartment on the third floor of MegaGamers. She is dismayed when Ping answers the door wearing only a t-shirt, and leaves thinking that Piro might not be such a nice guy after all. Container ships burn off the coast as Ed and Dom arrive in Japan.

Chapter 2: Things Change Little By Little... *published in: Megatokyo Volume 2*

Faced with rioting students who are demanding the return of Great Teacher Largo, Shiritsu Daitou High School sends Junpei to bring Largo back to teach his class. Kimiko auditions for the voice role of "Kotone" in a game called "Sight." Asmodeus shows up to tempt Piro and sabotage Seraphim's work. Miho mysteriously faints in the bathroom and Ping watches over her as she recovers in the nurse's office. Ed, whose mission it is to return Ping to the Sony labs, finds her but is thrown out the window when he tries to 'retire' her. The explosion caused by Ed's landing opens an inter-dimentional rift, unleashing an undead horde upon the city. Dom helps Largo fend off the zombie attack before the Tokyo Police shut everything down due to improper permits. Yuki returns to MegaGamers and asks Piro for art lessons. Later on, Erika startles Kimiko by inviting the boys out for drinks at a beer garden. As Largo details the day's exploits to to her, Erika watches as an inebriated Kimiko yells at an equally inebriated Piro. The night ends as Erika and Largo carry their unconcious roommates home.

Chapter 3: Am I Your Number One Fan? *published in: Megatokyo Volume 3*

Largo takes his class to an arcade to sharpen their skills, but loses a duel to Miho. Piro visits Kimiko at the Anna Miller's restaurant where she works. Largo is apprehended by Inspector Sonoda (Yuki's father) but the arrest is interrupted by the attack of a giant, drunken monster turtle. Largo cleverly uses Ping's strength to fend him off which impresses the Inspector, who hires him to be a Special Contract Operative for the Tokyo Police Cataclysm Division. Kimiko learns that she has won the role of Kotone in the game, "Sight." Piro gives Kimiko a drawing he had done of Kotone, one of his favorite characters. Piro forgets Yuki's art lesson as he does "research" to figure out what to do next about Kimiko.

Chapter 4: Low Ping Rate *published in: Megatokyo Volume 3*

Miho takes Ping and the boys out to a public bath and then to a restaurant where she reveals herself as their old nemesis from an online roleplaying game. Seraphim is captured by Asmodeus to prevent her from meddling with his plans to get Piro to loosen up and have more fun in Tokyo. Back at MegaGamers, Dom confronts Erika about her former idol singer career that she had abruptly abandoned, leaving her fans wanting more. Largo fends off a probing attack by fanboys in the digital plane and physically removes one who came to see if the rumors about Erika's whereabouts are true. Boo comes to the rescue and battles Asmodeus, but Seraphim is injured in the attempt. Yuki's brother Yuuji confirms that Erika is indeed the long missing Idol.

Chapter 5: Color Depth *published in: Megatokyo Volume 4*

A crowd of Erika's fans assemble outside MegaGamers. Largo brings his class to help fend them off. Erika prepares to face the mob, but Ed's new attempt on Ping's life shatters the area. Erika and Piro go outside to check on the mob's safety but retreat back inside when Piro is injured. Inspector Sonoda disperses the mob and explains the power idols have over the public and how Erika is still quite 'dangerous.' Kimiko frets over Piro who initially tries to hide from her but then faces his fears and goes to talk with her. Yuki, who has arrived for her lesson, leaves when she sees Piro and Kimiko's obvious concern for each other. Largo finds Erika curled up and depressed in the break room and works to cheer her up by challenging her to a video game.

Chapter 6: Operational Insecurity *published in: Megatokyo Volume 4*

Largo convinces Erika that she can better handle her fans if she monitors them online and gives her computer lessons. He follows her as she goes out to buy parts to make her own PC. They run into Sonoda Meimi, Yuki's mom and a woman Erika looks up to, who mistakes Largo as Erika's new boyfriend. A confused, bitter and conflicted Erika harshly tries to drive Largo away, but it backfires as Largo tells her that he refuses to play that game and leaves. Piro, depressed by how well Largo seems to be doing with Erika and how poorly he feels he is doing with Kimiko, blindly follows Ping to the Cave of Evil nightclub which Miho has invited them to record Kimiko's first radio appearance. Largo, who has drowned himself in beer, follows them. After being confronted by Ping and unable to hear Kimiko's show, Piro returns to the main floor only to find Miho cruelly messing with Largo. He confronts Miho and drags his friend out of the club. Kimiko's publicity appearance on the radio show doesn't go well after she scolds the hosts for badmouthing fans. All this is forgotten as she tries to help Piro get a drunk and skittish Largo home. Kimiko and Piro talk openly for the first time as Piro finally understands that constantly tearing himself down only hurts the people who care about him.

Chapter 7: Known Bugs and Security Flaws and **Chapter 8: Defect Mapping** are included in this book. Please note that this guide is no replacement for reading the comic. There are many small details and subtle things in the story that can't adequately be described in a synopsis.

Read the books and save your bandwidth, or visit **www.megatokyo.com** and start reading from the beginning.

Other Material

Megatokyo contains a lot of random material including OSE (One Shot Epsiodes), SGD (Shirt Guy Dom), DPD (Dead Piro Days) and GST (Guest Strips) which are not covered in this guide. There are two "Omake" (extra or bonus) short stories and two "Endgame" extras that are worth noting:

Endgames : Presence *published in: Megatokyo Volume 2*

A written short story (with 5 illustrations) that looks back at the adventures of Largo and Pirogoeth in the Endgames gameworld. Not available online, print version only.

Endgames : Disabled *published in: Megatokyo Volume 3*

Further adventures of Largo and Pirogoeth in the Endgames gameworld. Fully illustrated 8 page comic not available online, print version only.

Omake Theater: Grand Theft Colo: Otaku City *published in: Megatokyo Volume 3*

Makoto the MT server is kidnapped and on the run from all sorts of shady and vaguely familiar characters.

Omake Theater: Circuity *published in: Megatokyo Volume 4*

A haunting tale where Piro helps an injured girl with wings while Largo seeks a lost friend. Print version is a reworked and revised expansion of the original online Omake.

Megatokyo: Story Timeline

One problem with Megatokyo has always been the question: How long have Largo and Piro been in Tokyo? I was not very careful with the passage of time in Chapter 0, but since Chapter 1 each chapter has covered a single day. A few years ago i sat down and worked out an official timeline, and for this Readers' Guide we have researched, corrected, updated and finalized it.

Chapter 0: Relax, We Understand J00
Day 1 (Thursday, mid July) - Piro and Largo go to E3 [comics 001-006]
Day 2 (Saturday) - Piro and Largo arrive in Japan [comics 007-012]
Day 3 (Sunday) - Piro and Largo meet Tsubasa [comics 014-036]
Day 4-46 (Mondays) - Six weeks pass, Largo and Piro play games [comics 037-040]
Day 47 (Tuesday, early September) - Piro and Largo waste their ticket money [comic 041]
Day 48 (Wednesday) - Piro loses his bookbag, Yuki finds it [comics 042-060]
Day 49 (Thursday) - Piro gives his railcard to Kimiko [comics 061-074]
Day 50 (Friday) - Yuki sends Piro an e-mail but he deletes it [comics 075-079]
Day 52 (Sunday) - Piro gets a job at the store, Largo meets Miho [comics 080-129]
Chapter 1: Do You Want To Save Before You Quit?
Day 53 (Monday, mid September) - Largo becomes a teacher, Kimiko delivers dinner [comics 134-192]
Chapter 2: Things Change Little By Little...
Day 54 (Tuesday) - Kimiko auditions, Miho faints, zombies attack on wrong day [comics 196-301]
Chapter 3: Am I Your Number One Fan?
Day 55 (Wednesday) - Arcade duel, Piro visits Anna Miller's, Gameru attacks [comics 307-397]
Chapter 4: Low Ping Rate
Day 56 (Thursday) - Bath and confessions with Miho, fanboy recon, Seraphim is captured [comics 402-514]
Chapter 5: Color Depth
Day 57 (Friday) - Fanboy horde and aftermath [comics 526-633]
Chapter 6: Operational Insecurity
Day 58 (Saturday) - Computer lessons and shopping with Erika, Kimiko's radio appearance [comics 639-729]
Chapter 7: Known Bugs and Security Flaws
Day 59 (Sunday) - Fanboy mob at Anna Miller's, the truth of Erika's past revealed [comics 743-873)]
Chapter 8: Defect Mapping
Day 60 (Monday) - Kimiko quits, Erika builds her PC, Ping has a good cry [comics 875-968]

Character Guide

Piro　　ぴろ

Quiet, shy, introverted, fluent in Japanese, Piro is a huge fan of anime, manga and dating sim games. Currently employed by MegaGamers, he lives with Largo in the apartment on the third floor. Usually self-deprecating, but can be fiercely protective of his friends. Learned most of what he knows about life from Shoujo (Girls) Manga. Known game avatars: Piroko, Pirogoeth, Pirokiko, Pirokoro.

Largo　　ラルゴ

In Japan on a Mortal Combat visa. Currently employed as an English teacher at Shiritsu Daitou High School where he is known by students as "Great Teacher Largo." Worked briefly as a Tokyo Police Cataclysm Division Special Contract Operative. Designated as a threat to the balance of chaos in Japan by the TPCD. Energetic and boisterous, fiercely competitive, always fights with honor and is proud of his l33t skillz.

Nanasawa Kimiko　　七澤希　美子

Aspiring voice actress. Currently employed by the Meguro Anna Miller's restaurant and as a voice actress for Kotone in the much anticipated game "Sight." Her recent appearance on Mumu-chan's VoiceVoice Paradise radio show caused a huge stir in the fanboy community. Currently lives in Takaido with Hayasaka Erika. Very caring and has strong empathy, but often feels haunted by a deep sadness and inner turmoil.

Hayasaka Erika　　早坂　えりか

Former superstar idol singer and voice actress, most famous role was Moeko in the "Girl Phase" anime. Quit her career suddenly while still at the height of popularity. Currently employed by MegaGamers, where she worked in obscurity until her location was compromised to her still thriving fan collective. Currently lives in Takaido with Nanasawa Kimiko. Stoic and reserved, she hides deep emotional scars behind a strong facade that only two people in her life have been able to penetrate.

Ping　　ピングちゃん

Prototype Sony SEVS-44936 robot girl Playstation 2 accessory for use with Emotional Doll System games. Missing from Sony R&D facilities, currently lives in the apartment on the third floor of MegaGamers in the custody of Piro. Student at Shiritsu Daitou High School. Member of Largo's class, good friends with Tohya Miho. Capable of extreme strength, especially when angered. Appearance and personality are variable and depend on current play mode.

Sonoda Yuki　　園田　由紀

Student at Shiritsu Daitou Gakuen fuzoku chuugaku (attached middle school). Recently discovered that she has "magical girl" abilities. Bold, daring and perky but often sensitive and insecure. Daughter of Inspector Sonoda Masamichi. Sonoda-san has been arrested for shoplifting on two occasions but no charges were filed in either incident. Best friends with Mami and Asako.

Tohya Miho 凍耶　美穂

Dark, mysterious student at Shiritsu Daitou High School, yet has missed much due to unexplained illnesses. Usually ignored by the other students in Largo's class, she is often seen at the Cave of Evil dance club. Identified by Largo as "t3h 3v1l," "Zombie Queen" or "Undead Priestess." To Piro she is a strange Goth girl with whom he once had a strange online "relationship." Her true identity and purpose is an enigmatic mystery.

Seraphim セラフィム

Level 9 conscience operative with the Conscience Enforcement Authority (CEA) Special Counseling Division. Current primary assignment is Piro. Cares for Piro but is frequently exasperated by him. There are unconfirmed reports that Special Agent Seraphim has two sisters who are very similar in appearance to her. Passionate about her work, she has a weakness for kitties and is very sensitive to fashion faux pas.

Dom ドッム

Works for Sega Black Ops. Arrives in Japan after being blackmailed by Largo to send money. Current target of interest seems to be Hayasaka Erika, who he wants to bring under the 'protection' of Sega. Cunning, cold blooded and capable of instant violence. Fluent in Japanese. Has a soft spot for his Heckler & Koch MK23 SOCOM.

Ed エド

Member of Sony's Enforcement Division. Recently arrived in Japan. Believed to be hunting the missing SEVS-44936 EDS prototype with intent to destroy. Ultra-violent, takes great joy in blowing things up. Has a passion for advanced weaponry. Frequent user of the rather comprehensive Sony medical plan.

Junpei ジュンペイ

Ninja with the Ninja Corporation, often does work for various government agencies in Tokyo. After being defeated by Largo in Mortal Combat, Junpei seeks the 'way of l33t' from the l33t master. A "High Level" Ninja, Junpei follows a strict code of honor. Junpei is also an Origami master.

Asmodeus アスモデウス

Operative of the "other" organization and an old adversary of Seraphim's. Currently assigned to the Piro case. Narcissistic and overconfident, Asmodeus enjoys his work and finds that temptation comes naturally to him. Has a preference for shiny, sparkly shirts.

Megatokyo Readers' Guide

Boo ブー

Temporarily employed as a Conscience Operative with the Conscience Enforcement Authority (CEA) Special Counseling Division. Hired to assist Seraphim with her workload, current primary assignment is Largo. Previously worked in entertainment and gaming. Even though he feels he is in way over his head, Boo always does his best. Usually communicates by drawing pictures on sticky notes.

Sonoda Meimi 園田　芽美

Yuki's mother, married to Inspector Sonoda Masamichi, mother of two. She is a retired magical girl of great power, a fact kept secret from her son and daughter. For her own reasons, she secretly accepted a contract to neutralize Largo. Sonada-san has a penchant for very sharp knives and seems to have a habit of forgetting to pay for items while shopping.

Sonoda Masamichi 園田　雅道

Inspector with the Tokyo Police Cataclysm Division. Has a personal interest in keeping watch over Hayasaka Erika due to her past involvement with his family. Sonoda works hard to protect the safety of Tokyo and has worked to reduce unplanned cataclysms by 30% in the last year, 42% overall since taking the post 18 years ago.

Sonoda Yuuji 園田　裕二

Son of Sonoda Masamichi and Sonoda Meimi. Suspected of having connections to numerous obsession level 5+ fan groups. Skilled at tinkering with electronics, he often practices on the wide array of small electronic devices his sister Yuki seems to mysteriously aquire on a regular basis.

Teramoto Mami 寺本　真美

Student at Shiritsu Daitou Gakuen fuzoku chuugaku. Friend of Sonoda Yuki. Serious and a skeptic, Mami keeps an extensive and detailed diary of her and her friends' lives. Has been concerned about Yuki since the incident with the bookbag.

Kurabayashi Asako 倉林　麻子

Student at Shiritsu Daitou Gakuen fuzoku chuugaku. Friend of Sonoda Yuki. Cheerful and bubbly. Asako is rumored to have been involved romantically with an upperclassman. Energetic to the point of being annoying, Mami and Yuki can always count on her to be there for them no matter what.

Tsubasa つばさ

Piro's friend in Japan. Rumored to have some connection to the Sony Emotional Doll System project, may have been involved in the disappearance of the "Ping" prototype. Recently left the country for America to search for his "hatsu koi" (first love). Currently somewhere in Oklahoma.

Ibara Junko 伊原 順子

Student at at Shiritsu Daitou High School and Class President of Largo's class. Sometimes bossy, self righteous and a stickler for rules, she can also look past them and be concerned and caring. Once admitted to having a predilection for older men, is also rumored to practice enjo kosai, though this has never been proven. An only child, few of her friends know that her father is a raging alcoholic and she is all that holds her family together.

Sawatari Megumi 沢渡 めぐみ

Currently employed by the Meguro Anna Miller's. Good friends with Nanasawa Kimiko. Sawatari is also an aspiring voice actress. Has big dreams, but is very realistic about trying to achieve them. Lives with and supports her aged grandmother. Has a secret thing for Ninjas.

Ryouya Sayuri 料屋 さゆり

Character designer for the much anticipated game "Sight." Closely involved in the recording sessions for the game, she has become a strong advocate of Kimiko's take on the character "Kotone." She has done character design work on dozens of popular ren'ai games and is a well respected name in the industry.

Matsui Takeshi 松居 猛

Executive Producer at Lockart, currently producing the long awaited game "Sight." Brisk and always wanting to keep things moving, he is often exasperated with Kimiko's approach to her character. In spite of his misgivings, he finds that her performances 'get' to him and finds himself worried about her personally. Not used to dealing with seiyuu with such... unusual and forceful personalities.

Niidera Satsuki 新寺 さつき

Kimiko's agent at the Ippai Voice Talent Agency, responsible for managing all her work in the industry. She has had difficulty finding parts for Kimiko, and is often frustrated with Kimiko's impulsive nature.

Megatokyo - Volume 5 index

This book contains strips from Chapter 7 and Chapter 8, and includes extra material produced between August 2005 and February 2007. For more information and more comics, visit www.megatokyo.com

Page No.	Strip Title	Date	Online Strip ID
93	a powerful healer	2006-04-14	850
94	he was no l33ch	2006-04-28	851
95	the deepest, most 3v1l magic	2006-05-01	852
96	t3h 3v1l	2006-05-05	853
97	the little game is over	2006-05-08	854
98	idiot	2006-05-10	855
99	are you trying to save me?	2006-05-12	856
100	wounds from within	2006-05-15	857
101	c) yell at her and make her cry.	2006-05-17	858
102	a game not worth playing	2006-05-19	859
103	real girls do not have security	2006-05-24	861
104	more coffee?	2006-05-26	862
105	the purity of your attention	2006-05-29	863
106	a girl with a pure heart	2006-06-01	864
107	wrong answer	2006-06-06	865
108	normal channels	2006-06-09	867
109	cowards	2006-06-12	868
110	cute frills	2006-06-14	869
111	a corrupted save	2006-06-16	870
112	deserved	2006-06-19	871
113	regrets	2006-06-21	872
114	OSE: Tree-free, Clothing-free!	2005-09-02	755
	Chapter 08		
115	defect mapping	2006-06-28	875
116	grumpy and wussy	2006-06-30	876
117	filling in	2006-07-03	877
118	wasting away	2006-07-05	878
119	no time for a pity party	2006-07-07	879
120	inflation	2006-07-10	880
121	no threat detected	2006-07-12	881
122	letting out	2006-07-14	882
123	kind of jealous	2006-07-17	883
124	little spine	2006-07-26	886
125	Kimi-zilla	2006-07-28	887
126	little changes	2006-07-31	888
127	a failed containment	2006-08-09	891
128	break_fast	2006-08-11	892
129	repurposing	2006-08-14	893
130	you being you	2006-08-16	894
131	it's not going to build itself	2006-08-18	895
132	you look hungry	2006-08-21	896
133	help	2006-08-23	897
134	a tough one	2006-08-25	898
135	big mode	2006-08-28	899
136	size and fit	2006-08-30	900
137	boxes	2006-09-01	901
138	five times	2006-09-05	902
139	seem easy	2006-09-06	903
140	great responsibility	2006-09-11	905
141	fault	2006-09-13	906
142	clean up	2006-09-18	908
143	cover up	2006-09-20	909
144	find someone else	2006-09-22	910
145	necessary theatrics	2006-09-25	911
146	how i want to feel	2006-09-27	912
147	undocumented jumper settings	2006-10-02	913
148	static	2006-10-04	914
149	shaking a feeling	2006-10-06	915
150	generating static	2006-10-09	916
151	lets fix this thing	2006-10-11	917
152	a lack of r3sp3ct	2006-10-13	918
153	proper respect	2006-10-18	920
154	a difficult skill	2006-10-20	921
155	comfort level	2006-10-25	922
156	i should just tell her	2006-10-26	923
157	warm coffee	2006-10-29	924
158	standing out	2006-10-30	925
159	i'm not going to let you play	2006-11-01	926
160	hurt feelings	2006-11-03	927
161	grief this	2006-11-06	928
162	casualty report	2006-11-08	929
163	cry response	2006-11-10	930
164	inside information	2006-11-13	931
165	will you tell me?	2006-11-15	932
166	innocent	2006-11-17	933
167	real behaviour	2006-11-20	934
168	taken lightly	2006-11-22	935
169	monsters like us	2006-11-26	936
170	feed	2006-11-27	937
171	no one ever knows	2006-11-29	938
172	something wrong	2006-12-02	939
173	a fake one	2006-12-04	940
174	i don't want to be a fantasy	2006-12-06	941
175	disquieting	2006-12-09	942
176	looking up, looking down	2006-12-12	943
177	a good shift	2006-12-13	944
178	really bad	2006-12-15	945
179	(new page) - don't look	2007-02-21	n/a
180	nothing to be afraid of	2006-12-18	946
181	it is as i ph34r3d	2006-12-22	947
182	it's important to her	2006-12-30	949
183	a few error codes	2007-01-01	950

Page No.	Strip Title	Date	Online Strip ID
184	you can't turn her off	2007-01-03	951
185	the system won't boot	2007-01-06	952
186	come out right	2007-01-08	953
187	engage	2007-01-12	954
188	yes, we're fine	2007-01-15	955
189	what should i do?	2007-01-17	956
190	I must prepare for the journey	2007-01-20	957
191	rising to the challenge	2007-01-23	958
192	unable to drive fast	2007-01-25	959
193	you bother me	2007-01-29	961
194	it won't be that bad	2007-02-01	962
195	late night TV	2007-02-04	963
196	sniper rig	2007-02-06	964
197	a clean shot	2007-02-07	965
198	distracted	2007-02-09	966
199	good night	2007-02-12	967
200	disturbed	2007-02-14	968
201	Leave it to Seraphim: Your Health!	2006-06-26	874
	Shirt Guy Dom Strips		
203	SGD: Diarrhea of the Mouth	2005-08-22	750
204	SGD: Cubicle Defense	2006-03-24	837
205	SGD: Sticks on a Plane	2006-08-04	889
206	SGD: Anything to Declare?	2007-01-27	960
	Dead Piro Days		
208	YANRDPD: 5l<00l_ D4yz	2006-01-23	812
209	DPD: cutting losses	2006-02-13	820
210	DPD: Sonoda Yuki (Otakon 2005)	2005-08-17	748
211	DPD: pol3sitting	2006-07-19	884
212	in service DPD: chapter 7 - stuff not seen	2006-06-23	873
213	DPD random: Kimiko	2005-10-21	776
214	DPD: serious	2006-09-06	904
215	DPD: Largo, Legionnaire of Reaht	2006-10-16	919
216	DPD: b4k4.md7 reload	2005-11-24	790
217	DPD: such cute little bandaids	2006-03-03	828
218	Christmas 2006 - alternate image		n/a
219	Christmas 2006	2005-12-25	948
220	DPD: Piroko Sheepdog and Largo Wolf	2006-09-15	907
	"Two Weeks" DPD series		
222	two weeks DPD1: broken blades	2006-03-20	835
223	two weeks DPD2: tilting windmills	2006-03-22	836
224	two weeks DPD3: movement of air	2006-03-29	839
225	two weeks DPD4: stillness	2006-03-31	840

I Hate You More Than Anyone

By Banri Hidaka

Tomboy Kazuha keeps her feelings inside—until she meets the first guy who treats her like a girl.

July 2007

King of Cards

By Makoto Tateno

Manami is guided through a hit trading card game by the most powerful character in the deck—Sahgan the Sorcerer!

August 2007

The Palette of 12 Secret Colors

By Nari Kusakawa

Cello could be a great wizard—if she could just learn to control her power!

October 2007

Venus In Love

By Yuki Nakaji

College is a time to make friends, take trips, and fall in love... with many people.

November 2007

Tears of a Lamb

By Banri Hidaka

Life is hard, but friends can help you through it.

January 2008

CMX®

For more exciting CMX Manga, visit your local bookseller or call 1-888-COMICBOOK for the nearest comics shop. For more information and previews, visit cmxmanga.com

▶STOP!◀

This is the back of the book!

Oh dear. If you think this is the front of the book, you have been reading an unhealthy amount of manga. MEGATOKYO was originally done in English, so be a good dear and turn the book over and start from the other side.